D0783210

TRANSFORMING
OUR
WORLD
a Call to Action

James M Boice
EDITOR
TRANSFORMING
OUR
WORLD
a Call to Action

MULTNOMAH

10209 SE Division Street, Portland, Oregon 97266

Acknowledgments:
Chapter 9, "The Kingdom of God and Human Kingdoms" by Charles W.
Colson, is based on *Kingdoms in Conflict*, © 1987 by Charles Colson.
Copublished by William Morrow & Company and Zondervan Publishing
House. Used by permission.

Unless otherwise indicated, all Scripture quotations are from the Holy Bible:
New International Version, © 1973, 1978, 1984 by the International Bible
Society. Used by permission of Zondervan Bible Publishers.

Edited by Rodney L. Morris
Cover design by Bruce DeRoos

TRANSFORMING OUR WORLD
© 1988 by Multnomah Press
Portland, Oregon 97266

Multnomah Press is a ministry of Multnomah School of the Bible, 8435
Northeast Glisan Street, Portland, Oregon 97220.

Printed in the United States of America.

All rights reserved. No part of this publication may be reproduced, stored
in a retrieval system, or transmitted, in any form or by any means, electronic,
mechanical, photocopying, recording, or otherwise, without the prior written
permission of the publisher.

Library of Congress Cataloging-in-Publication Data

Transforming our world.

   1. Church and the world—Congresses.   2. Church and
social problems—United States—Congresses.
3. Church and state—United States—Congresses.
4. United States—Moral conditions—Congresses.
I. Boice, James Montgomery
BR115.W6T69   1988
ISBN 0-88070-222-2 pbk.)

88 89 90 91 92 93 94 95 - 10 9 8 7 6 5 4 3 2 1

Contents

To Him
Who Alone Shall Reign
Forever and Ever
Amen

Preface

The International Council on Biblical Inerrancy
1978-1987

What Scripture says, God says—
through human agents and without error.

The essays in this volume were prepared as plenary addresses for Congress on the Bible II, a gathering of thirty-one hundred Christian laypersons and pastors, who met in Washington, D.C., September 23-27, 1987, at the call of the International Council on Biblical Inerrancy, which planned and sponsored the event.

The International Council on Biblical Inerrancy came into being at the end of 1977 and the beginning of 1978 with a decade-long program to combat a drift away from the classical, high view of the Bible and biblical authority perceived to be occurring even in so-called evangelical churches and institutions. At one of its early meetings, the council adopted the following statement as an expression of its purpose:

THE SITUATION

1. Even among evangelicals, Christian doctrine and Christian living are moving progressively away from the Bible's standard and from the classical teaching of the church.

9

2. This tragic departure is directly related to the denial in many quarters of the historical doctrine of the verbal inerrancy of the Bible.

3. Large portions of evangelical scholarship, which have accepted many of the negative critical theories of the writing of the Bible and a neo-orthodox approach to revelation, are endeavoring to redefine evangelicalism after their own image.

4. Most laymen, Christian leaders, and pastors seem to be theologically unequipped to discern this departure from the historic view of the Bible or to see the vast consequences which tend to follow from that departure.

5. Because of a contemporary unbiblical view of love and low evaluation of truth, many evangelicals who are alerted to this doctrinal departure tend optimistically to think the problem will somehow vanish. Or they find themselves emotionally resistant to any effort to have the issues clarified, which might result in referring to some brothers and sisters as unbiblical.

In light of the situation we see, and in response to the burden it has placed on our hearts, we commit ourselves to this purpose:

OUR PURPOSE

To take a united stand in elucidating, vindicating, and applying the doctrine of biblical inerrancy as an essential element for the authority of Scripture and a necessity for the health of the church of God, and to attempt to win the church back to this historical position.

During the next ten years ICBI and its objectives were richly blessed by God. The organization published many volumes of academic and lay literature on the Bible and Bible-related themes; held regional "Authority of Scripture" seminars throughout the United States; conducted three "Summit" meetings on the subjects of "Inerrancy" (1978), "Hermeneutics" (1982), and the "Application of the Bible to Contemporary Issues" (1986); and two large lay conferences, one in San Diego in 1982 and one in Washington in 1987.

During those years the literature produced by ICBI has been disseminated around the world; similar, supportive organizations have been founded; and the three "Affirmation and Denial" statements have achieved almost creedal stature in some quarters. The council believes that many have been recalled to the highest standards of biblical authority by these efforts and that what has been accomplished will continue to bear fruit for years to come.

With the completion of Congress on the Bible II, ICBI came to the end of its ten-year program. It ceased to exist. The charge it believed it had received from God is now being passed to other hands.

ICBI's work has taken it through three stages: (1) a defense of the Bible's full authority, (2) an exploration of the proper principles of biblical interpretation, and (3) the application of the Bible's teaching, properly interpreted, to today's problems. This last stage brought it into close contact with those many evangelical organizations, scores of which were present in Washington for Congress on the Bible II, which have held to the Bible's full authority and inerrancy and have been attempting to apply its teachings and standards to our culture. ICBI therefore encourages you, the supporters of ICBI and the readers of this volume, to link hands with these front-line Christian organizations and support them with your own time, talents, and resources.

CONTRIBUTORS TO THIS VOLUME

The authors of the chapters in this volume are:

Senator William Armstrong. Senator Armstrong is the United States Senator from Colorado. He has served two terms in the Senate and before that was a three-term Congressman. He is the ranking Republican on the Senate Budget Committee and Chairman of the Subcommittee on Social Security and Income Maintenance. He is well known in Washington for his Christian faith.

James Montgomery Boice. Dr. Boice is Senior minister of Tenth Presbyterian Church, Philadelphia, Pennsylvania; president of Evangelical Ministries, Inc.; speaker on the international radio program "The Bible Study Hour"; and author of more than thirty-five theology and Bible study books. He was the Chairman of the International Council on Biblical Inerrancy.

William F. Buckley, Jr. Mr. Buckley is Founder and Editor of the *National Review*, author of the syndicated newspaper column "On the Right," host of the popular television program "Firing Line," and a prolific author. He has been a presidential appointee to the United States Information Agency, the United Nations, and the National Security Council.

Charles W. Colson. Mr. Colson is Chairman of the Washington, D.C. based Prison Fellowship Ministry, which has fostered action in prison ministry, sentencing, and prison reform in the United States and around the world. He is the author of *Born Again*, *Life Sentence*, *Loving God*, *Kingdoms in Conflict*, and other works. He was the Chairman of Congress on the Bible II.

Os Guinness. Mr. Guinness is a Guest Scholar with The Brookings Institute, Washington, D.C. For five years he worked with Dr. Francis Schaeffer at the L'Abri Fellowship in Switzerland. He is the author of *The Dust of Death*, *In Two Minds*, and *The Gravedigger File*.

Richard John Neuhaus. Dr. Neuhaus is Director of the Rockford Institute Center on Religion and Society, New York, and editor of its periodicals *Religion and Society Report* and *This World: A Journal of Religion and Public Life*. He is best known for his books, *The Naked Public Square*, *The Catholic Moment*, and others.

James I. Packer. Dr. Packer is Professor of Systematic and Historical Theology, Regent College, Vancouver, British

Columbia, and the author of such well-known volumes as *Fundamentalism and the Word of God*, *Evangelism and the Sovereignty of God*, *Knowing God*, and *Beyond the Battle for the Bible*. He was a member of the Planning Committee for Congress on the Bible II.

John M. Perkins. Dr. Perkins is Founder and President of the John M. Perkins Foundation for Reconciliation and Development, Pasadena, California; and Founder and President Emeritus of Voice of Calvary Ministries, Jackson, Mississippi. He served on President Ronald Reagan's Task Force on Food Assistance and the Private Sector Initiative Program.

R. C. Sproul. Dr. Sproul is President of Ligonier Ministries, Orlando, Florida, and Professor of Systematic Theology and Apologetics at Reformed Theological Seminary, Jackson, Mississippi. He is the author of many books including *The Holiness of God*, *The Intimate Marriage*, and *Chosen by God*. He was an original member of the International Council on Biblical Inerrancy.

James Montgomery Boice
Philadelphia, Pennsylvania

PART 1

DEFINING THE TASK

Chapter 1

One Nation under God

James Montgomery Boice

*T*hese are critical days in our nation's history. In 1984, in the course of the last presidential campaign, President Ronald Reagan said, "Just about every place you look, things are looking up. Life is better—America is back—and people have a sense of pride they never thought they'd feel again." But only four months ago, after the upheavals of the Iran-Contra affair, the insider-trading scandals on Wall Street, and the revelations of misconduct in the lucrative evangelical television industry, *Time* magazine wrote perceptively, "America, which took such a back-thumping pride in its spiritual renewal, [now] finds itself wallowing in a moral morass." *Time* asked sharply, "Has the mindless materialism of the '80s left in its wake a values vacuum?"[1]

The Values Vacuum

A values vacuum is what we are dealing with, of course. But it is not something that has suddenly burst upon us in the 1980s. It has been with us (and growing) for a long, long time.

Dr. Francis Schaeffer, a founding member of the International Council on Biblical Inerrancy, traced our values crisis to the thought of Georg Wilhelm Friedrich Hegel, the German philosopher who invented the idea of the "historical dialectic." Hegel believed that history is always in a state of development. At any one period there may be something that a majority of the people agree on and are willing to regard as truth. Hegel called this a "thesis." But this "truth" is always countered by a contradictory idea, which Hegel called an "antithesis." And the result is a struggle between the "thesis" and the countering "antithesis" through which a new "truth" or "synthesis" develops. This new "truth" becomes the new "thesis," and the process repeats itself indefinitely. If this is the way things are, there can never be any absolute truth but only what is truth for you (but not necessarily for me) or me (but not necessarily for you). And what is truth today was not necessarily true yesterday and probably will not be true tomorrow.

The majority of our contemporaries live in this philosophical house, whether or not they realize they are Hegelians. For them, truth is relative. And where truth is relative there can be no absolutes. There can be no valid values.

In the last few years I have noticed that even secular writers have begun to mourn this missing element. One who has done so brilliantly is Allan Bloom, author of the recent best- selling critique of American higher education, *The Closing of the American Mind*. Bloom, a professor at the University of Chicago, does not have a Christian answer to the problem. This is the great and unfortunate omission in the book. He calls only for a return to classical learning, at least for a small core of intellectuals. But Bloom sees the problem clearly, and he has analyzed where it has come from and where it is going. In the very first lines he states: "There is one thing a professor can be absolutely certain of: almost every student entering the university believes, or says he believes, that truth is relative."[2]

If that is so, then there is no point in pursuing truth, no point in asking what is right as opposed to what is wrong, and the result is a downward spiral which has more in common with the first chapter of the book of Romans than the ever-popular Western or American ideal of "human progress."

In a July issue of the *National Review*, Secretary of Education William J. Bennett has courageously exposed the "value neutral" stance of our public schools' sex education programs as a factor in the alarming rise of teenage pregnancies in the last decade. According to Bennett, sex *does* involve values—absolute values—and we are harming our children by failing to say so. "We should recognize that sexual behavior is a matter of character and personality and that we cannot be value-neutral about it. Neutrality only confuses children and may lead them to conclusions we wish them to avoid." Instead of the values morass in the area of sex education, Bennett rightly says that we should teach children "sexual restraint as a standard to uphold and follow."[3]

The International Council on Biblical Inerrancy was created to fight the relativism of our culture, particularly in the church where it has spread. We have argued that Hegel is wrong and that our entire civilization is on a disastrously wrong path. We cannot survive without absolutes. But because we can never discover a basis for ultimate truth or absolutes in ourselves, we must receive these from God who has provided them for us in the pages of the Bible. That is where we learn who we are, who we are meant to be, who God is, how we can be reconciled to God through faith in Jesus Christ, and what God requires of us as Christ's followers.

I liked the title one of our television networks chose for a prime-time special on the recent visit of Pope John Paul to the United States. It was called "God Is Not Elected." We need to say that as Christians. God is not elected. Nor are right moral values. Values cannot be determined by the freedom of personal choice or a 51 percent vote.

Politics: A Misplaced Confidence

A second reason why these are crisis days for our country touches on the practices of evangelicals particularly. Either we have detached ourselves from the problems of our country, believing that the political system and the government that flows from it are so corrupt that no true Christian should have anything to do with them—an error more characteristic of the past—or else we have become so enamored with the political process that we have been swept up into the idolatrous notion that the Kingdom of God can come by political involvement. We need to repudiate both errors and work to articulate the correct roll of Christians as Christians in a secular state.

This is a worthy goal, but where should we start?

Here are five balanced statements to keep in mind as we begin:

1. Church and state must be separate from each other, in the sense that the church must not control national policy nor the state either establish or limit the free exercise of religion. But this does not mean that the state is independent of God or that either church or state is unanswerable to the other for how it carries out its functions.

The doctrine of the separation of church and state means that presidents are not to appoint clerics, define doctrine or establish church polity, and clerical authorities are not to appoint presidents or do the state's work. Nevertheless, church and state are both responsible to God in whose wisdom each has been established. Each is to remind the other of its God-appointed duties and recall it to upright, godly conduct if it strays. If Christians do not do their job of speaking to the civil authorities on moral issues, spiritual and moral principles will be eliminated from public debate, the state will become its own god, and the only functioning political principle will be pragmatism. This is precisely what has been happening in the United States in recent years.

2. Christians are free to seek elected office, and some should be encouraged to do so. But elected officials do not have to be Christians to be effective leaders, and merely being a Christian does not in itself qualify one for any office.

The Westminster Confession of Faith in its chapter on the "Civil Magistrate" states rightly that "it is lawful for Christians to accept and execute the office of a magistrate." This means that it is as proper for Christians to engage in secular pursuits, such as politics, as to become missionaries and ministers. But while missionaries and ministers must be born again to perform their function, civil leaders do not have to be. A Christian does not have to vote for the "Christian" candidate if a choice is offered, and he or she can pray for and support an unbeliever of good character and ability with both thankfulness and enthusiasm. Moreover, since none of us is able to see into another person's heart, if we think that we have to vote only for Christian candidates, we subject ourself to base manipulation by whatever candidate is willing to use the proper evangelical terms when speaking to us.

3. The Bible gives Christians guidelines for approaching national and social problems, and Christians will seek to be consistently biblical in all their thoughts and actions. But the Bible does not necessarily give specific answers to problems, and reasoning from a biblical principle to a specific public policy must be carefully done.

It is a valid complaint of seasoned politicians that many Christians leap too quickly from a valid truth of Scripture to a specific program and are overly hasty in denouncing anyone who disagrees with their program as being unbiblical or anti-God. If Christians are to gain a hearing in the rough and tumble of the political arena, they must be willing to fill in the gaps, showing how a suggested program best expresses and advances the desired principle. Moreover, Christians must argue their case with unbelievers, appealing to them on behalf of what is good for them and society and not retreating into an unassailable citadel of "revelation."

As Chuck Colson said recently, we "must equip and mobilize Christians, not to march down Pennsylvania Avenue, but effectively to bring biblical principles to bear on the mainstream issues of our culture."

4. In attempting to advance a specific proposal Christians must depend on moral suasion, asking God through prayer to give their reasoning favor with those having different points of view. They must not retreat from this high calling to tactics of mere naked pressure or coercion.

It is tempting to resort to such pressure. The political process is slow, riddled with compromise, and frustrating. It is tempting to try to short cut the hard work. Again, there are people who know only the tactics of public demonstration, economic boycott, media hype and back room power politics. Since these things often work for others, the Christian activist reasons that they should also work for him. And sometimes they do, although the results are frequently unsubstantial. Christians must not forget that the only truly lasting reforms come from God and that they have usually been a product of periods of great spiritual awakening.

5. Christians must think, work and pray effectively, trying always to place their specific programs within the framework of an overall Christian world and life view. But they must also strive no less personally to model the reality suggested.[4]

How Real Is Our Religion?

Can we do that? Will Christian people do it? In my opinion that question leads to the most important reason for the crisis before us and to our greatest challenge. For it is a way of saying that in the final analysis our problems are neither primarily philosophical or programmatic but are spiritual. As Aleksandr Solzhenitsyn said in London a few years ago on the occasion of his receiving the coveted Templeton Prize, "These things [the evils he had observed in the Soviet Union and the evils of the West as well] have happened to us because we have forgotten God."

We like to think of America as a religious nation. But American religion is shallow, and it is increasingly difficult to believe that most of it is achieving a lasting impact on society.

Several years ago, George Gallup, Jr., President of the American Institute of Public Opinion, reported on the nation's religious life in an address entitled "Is America's Faith for

Real?" His studies had shown that 81 percent of Americans consider themselves religious (only Italians, with 83 percent, rate higher). Nearly all Americans believe in God, and 71 percent believe in life after death. Well over three-fourths believe in heaven, and an astonishing two-thirds believe in hell. Large numbers believe in the Ten Commandments. Nearly every home has a Bible. Almost all pray. More than half of all Americans can usually be found in church on Sunday morning.

But these statistics are misleading. For, as Gallup also reported in the same address:

1. Only one person in five says that religion is the *most* influential factor in his or her life,
2. Although most Americans want religious education of some sort for their children, religious faith ranks far below many other traits that their parents would like to see developed in them, and
3. Only one person in eight says he or she would even consider sacrificing everything for God.

Gallup's surveys showed glaring ignorance of the Ten Commandments, even though we profess to believe in them; high levels of credulity (for example, high proportions of Americans, even churchgoers, believe in astrology); lack of basic spiritual disciplines; and a strong anti-intellectual bias where religious ideas are concerned. Americans want private emotional experiences rather than sustained, rigorous thought and the challenge of applying strong biblical values to their personal and public lives.[5]

John R. W. Stott, Rector Emeritus of London's All Souls Church, calls Western Christianity "skin-deep." He asks, "How can we have so many people claiming to be born again and yet have so little impact on society?"[6]

I was moved by what columnist William Reel wrote a decade ago for the New York *Daily News*. In an item entitled "Mean Street . . . X-Rated Streets," Reel cited the terrible statistics at that time—400,000 alcoholics, 500,000 narcotics users, 300,000 compulsive gamblers, over 600,000 felonies in the preceding year (assaults, robberies, muggings, rapes, murders)—in New York City alone. But then came his bottom line, a surprising three paragraph conclusion that asked for spiritual renewal.

> You gave up on New York politicians long ago. They are pathetic and embarrassing. But what is worse than the abdication of political leadership in New York is the abdication of spiritual leadership. There is no one willing to speak the truth, to call the Neros to account, to warn of the wrath of God.
>
> When was the last time a Catholic leader said anything more forceful than "God bless you"? New York needs a John the Baptist and Catholicism gives us Caspar Milquetoasts. The Protestant leadership is effete and insipid, debating Holy Orders for lesbians at a time when grandmothers are regularly and brutally assaulted by muggers and rapists. The Jewish establishment is moribund. Jeremiah must weep when, looking down from above, he contemplates these sad sacks sitting in their studies composing Passover messages that have no more spiritual content than a press release from the Liberal Party.
>
> New York was a great city when it put a great emphasis on spiritual values. Maybe we can get back to this. . . . Let's hope so. It can't happen a moment too soon. A beginning has got to be made immediately.[7]

A Much-Needed Text

What we need to do is spelled out in the text that the planning committee of Congress on the Bible II wisely chose as its theme verse—Micah 6:8.

He has showed you, O man, what is good.
And what does the LORD require of you?
To act justly and to love mercy
and to walk humbly with your God.

That verse is frequently quoted as if it were listing God's requirements for secular rulers, who, of course, are to provide for justice and show mercy. But it is actually a challenge to God's people to model what they recommend to others.

The verses immediately before this (vv. 6-7) contain four questions asked by the ungodly but religious inhabitants of Jerusalem to the effect that they were willing to do anything God might require of them—if only he would make his desires known. Does he want "burnt offerings . . . calves a year old"? That can be arranged. Does he want "thousands of rams," perhaps "ten thousand rivers of oil"? The people are willing to bring those. Perhaps God wants the "firstborn" children? The text suggests that the people might even be willing to offer their children to God, as their pagan neighbors had been doing. Throughout this entire prophecy God has been faulting those who profess the name of God for unrighteousness. But they come back to God with the arrogant suggestion that the fault is not theirs but God's. It is because God has not been explicit. "Tell us what we haven't done," they demand. The implication is that they are far more ready to serve God than he is to reveal his requirements.

So God answers them, and what he says is not new. He does not lay down further religious ordinances. All he asks is what he has asked from the beginning. And it is not ritual. It is not mere verbal assent. It is not even sacrificial giving to religious causes. It is:

To act justly,
To love mercy, and
To walk humbly with God.

To act justly does not mean merely to talk about justice or to get other people to act justly. It means to do the just thing yourself. Moreover, it means to do it, if necessary, over a long period of time.

There are two problems here. The first is knowing what the just thing is. This is not as easy as some people think. Is the just thing simply what the laws of the land require? It must be related to law, of course. But laws can be unjust, oppressive. They can be tools of favored classes to control those less favored. But how can we be sure that a given law is unjust? Are we able to make that determination by our own intellectual and moral powers? That might be possible if we were not sinful. But we are sinful. Our judgments are clouded by our own self-interest, and we ourselves become tools of what is wrong.

I have a friend who has served in the Philadelphia police department for twenty years and whose experiences in law enforcement have made him cynical. We have often talked about justice. But he has known of innumerable cases in which the guilty have gone free and the innocent have been punished. His testimony is: "On earth there is no such thing as justice."

The only way we can begin to know what justice is and act on it is if God, the author of justice, directs us in the correct way through Scripture, enabling us to see, not only the world but ourselves in that mirror.

The second problem is perseverance. It is one thing to know what justice is. That is hard enough. But even when we know what the just thing is, it is still difficult to establish justice, and we get tired in the attempt.

I was speaking to a student group at the University of Pennsylvania, stressing the kind of leadership needed in our nation's cities today, and a senior student approached me to object that he had been working in city politics and had found the situation so frustrating that he quit. He thought my talk had been too optimistic, that I was naive. I asked how old he was. He was twenty-two. I asked how long he has been involved in the political system. He replied that he had been involved for eighteen months. I said, "You are not old enough nor have you worked in the system long enough to be frustrated." And I say the same thing to myself. I have been working in Philadelphia for almost twenty years, but I have no more right to be frustrated than that student.

One of my associates says, "We tend to overestimate what God is going to accomplish in one year and underestimate what he is going to accomplish in twenty years." I think that is right. God takes the long view. Our responsibility is to act justly and work for justice, however long it takes.

The second requirement is *to love mercy*. This does not mean merely that we are to love mercy in others or even to act in a merciful way here and there or from time to time. It means that we are to show mercy in concrete ways and to do so consistently.

That is why a social service project was part of the program of Congress on the Bible II. We are not pretending that what we accomplished in the few days we were in Washington was a major contribution to overcoming the awesome social needs of that city. But it was a way of modeling what we say needs to be done. Words are not enough. To be merciful means to be loving, kind, and gracious to other people. But it also means to help them physically and financially.

We believe what the apostle James said when he wrote in James 2:14-19,

> What good is it, my brothers, if a man claims to have faith but has no deeds? Can such faith save him? Suppose a brother or sister is without clothes and daily food. If one of you says to him, "Go, I wish you well; keep warm and well fed," but does nothing about his physical needs, what good is it? In the same way, faith by itself, if it is not accompanied by action, is dead.
>
> But someone will say, "You have faith; I have deeds."

Show me your faith without deeds, and I will
show you my faith by what I do. You believe that
there is one God. Good! Even the demons believe
that—and shudder.

The final requirement expressed in Micah 6:8 is *to walk
humbly with God*. Have you known Christians who are anything
but humble in the way they go about their business? I am sure
you have. Such people think they have all the answers, when
they do not, and they rightly bring the world's scorn upon
themselves. We do not have all the answers. We must begin
by saying that. At best we are part of the solution, and we may
even be part of the problem. Besides, if by the grace of God
we are able to accomplish anything for good in the midst of
the present crisis situation, it will be in precisely that way: by
the grace of God. And this means that it is God's work, not
ours. It is God's kingdom. We are only servants of the King
of that kingdom. If that is so, how can we who know we are
sinners be anything but humble. How can we desire anything
but to walk humbly with God?

Before the Watching World

The world is waiting for us to do that. It is waiting for
Christians to be Christians. You say, "I don't believe that. I try
to bear witness to my non-Christian friends, and they don't
even want to hear about Christianity." Well, that is true. They
are unsaved people. They do not want to be reconciled to God.
That is part of what it means to be in an unsaved condition.
But they do want you to be what you profess to be as a Christian,
and they expect to see good come from it. The world looks to
Christians for far more than we give it credit for.

I mentioned earlier a Gallup poll on the religious life of
America. Here is another. Co-sponsored by the Charles F. Ket-
tering and Charles Stuart Mott Foundations, the Gallup organization surveyed more than three thousand urban residents eighteen years of age and over, asking what city entities they perceived as trying most "to improve city life." It was a great list.

It included the mayor, the city council, the local newspapers, local service groups, neighborhood groups, the Chamber of Commerce, local retail merchants, television stations, radio stations, city banks, small companies, major companies, "the company you work for," local labor unions, the advertising industry, and so on. Do you know what organization topped the list of those perceived as trying hardest to improve city life? The local churches! They received 48 percent of the vote. And the next highest on the list was the mayor, and he or she only received 39 percent.

And while I am at it, let me go back to that original Gallup poll that showed how shallow the religious faith and knowledge of most Americans really is. Because the statistics seemed so basically contradictory—many who claimed to be religious but who seemed to know and care so little about true Christian faith— Gallup devised a scale to sort out those for whom religion really did seem to be important. They were the one in eight who really would consider sacrificing everything for their religious beliefs or God. Gallup called them "the highly spiritually committed."

What about these people? Gallup discovered that, unlike the others, they were a "breed apart," different from the rest of the population in at least four key respects.

1. They are more satisfied with their lot in life than those who are less spiritually committed—and far happier. Two-thirds say they are "very happy" as compared with only 30 percent of those who are uncommitted.
2. Their families are stronger. The divorce rate among this group is far lower than among the less committed.
3. They tend to be more tolerant of persons of different races and religions than those who are less spiritually committed. That is exactly the opposite of what the media suggest when handling religion or religious figures.

And here is the most striking finding of all . . .

4. They are far more involved in charitable activities than are their counterparts. A total of 46 percent of the highly spiritually committed say they are presently working among the poor, the infirm, and the elderly, compared to only 36 percent among the moderately committed, 28 percent among the moderately uncommitted, and 22 percent among the highly uncommitted.[8]

We need to be reminded that genuine conversion does make profound differences in a person's life. And it is just those persons the country needs. Laws change nothing. People do. And the only thing that ever really changes people is God himself through the gospel of our Lord Jesus Christ. So let us get on with our calling.

Our King is Jesus.
Our marching orders are the Bible.
Our tactics are obedience, prayer, and service.
Our goals are the goals of God's kingdom.

There are times in history when it takes a thousand voices to be heard as one voice. But there are other times, times like our own, when one can ring forth as a thousand. Today the people of the United States of America are desperate for leadership. Let those who claim to know God act justly, love mercy, and walk humbly with God—for the good of all.

Chapter 1, Notes

1. *Time*, 25 May 1987, 14.
2. Allan Bloom, *The Closing of the American Mind* (New York: Simon and Schuster, 1987), 25.
3. William J. Bennett, "Why Johnny Can't Abstain," *National Review*, 3 July 1987, 36-38, 56.
4. See James Montgomery Boice, "Five Basics for Political Involvement," *Eternity*, September 1987, 18.
5. George Gallup, Jr., "Is America's Faith for Real?" *Princeton Theological Seminary Alumni News*, Summer 1982, 15-17.
6. "Taking Aim Against Skin-Deep Christianity: An Interview with John Stott" in *RTS*, Reformed Theological Seminary's alumni newsletter, Summer 1987, 8.
7. *The New York Daily News*, 1 April 1977.
8. Gallup, "America's Faith," 16.

Chapter 2

The Inseparability of Church and State

William F. Buckley, Jr.

You should know that I am a Roman Catholic, that I was was raised in the faith and live comfortably in it—however uneven my compliance with its higher demands—and that I hold my commitment to Christian truths to be the singular obligation as also the singular blessing in my life.

You should know also that I am happiest as an American. I attempt to say this in such a way as to avoid what might otherwise sound as mere patriotic bombast. Accordingly, I add that I could probably manage to be happy as a Swiss, but only if I could learn to dominate one of the languages spoken there. I suppose I could have been happy in England or Ireland, though emigration there would be difficult for all the obvious reasons, and for some less obvious, among them, the irritating nature of other countries' eccentricities. Our own, we are accustomed to. I can hear the awful melody of our national anthem and still feel my heart pounding with pride; but I would find it most awfully difficult to curtsy to the queen.

An Acute Separation

Why should we be so inflamed to stress the separateness of church and state? The argument is well known, and universally accepted, against establishing a single religion at the expense of others, though it is perhaps worth remarking that established religion in England has not for one hundred years meant privations for competing denominations. On the other hand, the established religion in England has not meant very much to most Englishmen. The last figures I saw suggest that only about 10 percent of the English commune regularly with their established church, the balance confining their association with it to baptisms, marriages, and funerals.

The question that accosts us in America is: Why is it that what has evolved from the First Amendment has taken us so much further than merely a reiteration of the traditional resolve to separate the church and state? What we have endured is a series of progressively incapacitating gestures, most of them propelled by the courts, that go beyond separation and argue an inchoate incompatibility between church and state.

It was only thirty-five years ago that a Supreme Court Justice, William Douglas, wrote in an opinion, "We are a religious people whose institutions presuppose a Supreme Being." If Judge Bork had written these words, he would probably have been disqualified at first sight for service in the Supreme Court.

We recognize, then, a political development, the progressive estrangement of government and religion. This has been done by a series of complicated, not to say incoherent, prohibitions ranging from the refusal to grant released time for religious studies to a refusal to permit the display of simulacra of the scene at Bethlehem to adorn public properties. Oh, there are the exceptions, but one suspects that the survival of Thanksgiving and of the chaplains in Congress is owing to the courts' conviction that on Thanksgiving few actually pause to give thanks to God; and to their conviction that at the opening of congressional sessions, no one listens to—let alone is guided by—what the preachers preach.

Now it is too early to say whether judicial hostilities, which date back to the distortion by Hugo Black in 1947 in the Everson decision of the intentions of the drafters of the First Amendment, will have the effect of causing an attrition in formal Christianity in America. The data are confusing. On the one hand—and here I speak of my own church—there is a sharp decline in the number of religious schools, perhaps directly related, perhaps unrelated, to the decline in religious vocations and in church attendance. On the other hand, there are signs in the Christian community of the quite stubborn refusal, so much desired by the agnostic community, to evanesce. After all, the church grew in the catacombs; and Christianity flourishes, of all places, in Poland, a Communist state. If we can't handle the Supreme Court and People for the American Way, perhaps we do not deserve to survive. But that is only the institutional point.

The second question asks not whether Christianity is the victim of institutional prejudice, but whether there are subtle forces at work, the design of which is to erode the ethical postulates of America, the very idea of which, to quote Justice Douglas, presupposes a Supreme Being. A Supreme Being who spoke to us in the Bible—a point worth making, one supposes, since for all our talk about pluralism, there is no serious contention here for religious primacy between the Judeo-Christian community and, say, the Hindi or the Muslim communities. The primacy of the Bible is what we are talking about. And even as the authors of the Federalist Papers agreed that the objective is nothing less than to revive an ethos, even as the Federalist papers agreed that there would be a separation of church and state, so they argued that a republic would endure only as long as it cultivated a virtuous people. So we have always needed, and will always need, to define what it is that characterizes a virtuous people. And to know this, we believe it is necessary to consult the Bible. It is the nation's umbilical cord to the definition of virtue.

A while ago, contemplating the failure of our national drug control program, I advocated licensing drug sales alongside a national educational effort to persuade potential drug users on purely utilitarian grounds that on the whole they were better off not amputating mind and body in exchange for quick, nervous highs. None of the reactions to my suggestion surprised me (I do not mean to disdain the routine objections, merely to note that they were anticipated)—with one exception. That objection was given by Dr. Mitchell Rosenthal, writing in *Newsweek*. He is the head of Phoenix House. He said that drugs should continue to be illegal, pending the day when they were universally shunned, explaining that the only way to lick marijuana—he targeted that particular drug merely as an example—was to engender what he called "societal disapproval" and to bring on what he called "informal social sanctions" of a kind that would make marijuana simply unacceptable. His objective is nothing less than to "revive an ethos," to make drug taking "sinful."

What exactly does that mean?

The development of an ethos is something that can indeed be achieved. Two examples come to mind.

I do not tire of recalling the distinguished and scholarly Bostonian who told me one day at lunch that he would today stand up and leave the room if he heard spoken any of the casual anti-Semitic remarks he routinely heard spoken as a boy in the dining room of his distinguished father. Americans sixty years old or older have lived through a period during which lackadaisical anti-Semitism all but disappeared. It happened almost as suddenly as the anachronisation of the word *Negro*. Nobody is a Negro any more except maybe the United Negro College Fund.

The second example of an evolutionized taboo has to do with garbage on coastal waters. One does not, in sight of land, throw garbage off one's boat into the sea. You can take the most disorderly, self-indulgent twenty-one-year-old out sailing. He may smoke pot in his cabin below while fornicating, but he will not throw his trash overboard. How come? Something moral in character became vitalized or revitalized.

Why and by what? In the matter of anti-Semitism, one

can hardly ask for a more melodramatic propulsive agent of racial tolerance than the Holocaust. With the exception of the Arab world (inflamed as it is by irredentist and other passions) and the Communist world (shaped in part by an ideology xenophobically hospitable to the notion that the "cosmopolitanism" of the Jews endangers the socialist movement) the impact of anti-Semitism run rampant under the Nazis burrowed into the sensibilities of the moral style setters in our culture and, through them, pretty much to the population at large—always excepting the exceptions.

In the matter of a respect for conservation, the whole idea of the vulnerable planet worked its way into the agenda of common concerns, especially among young college people. It was, to be sure, one part fad; but it was also one part dogma. And dogmas, strictly defined, tend to reflect attitudes about sin.

The moral theologians of yesteryear used the term, *ut in pluribus* to tell us that moral laws, if they hoped to grip the moral imagination, needed to be popularly plausible. And I am here saying that the fear and loathing of racial genocide, as of a ravaged planet, have actually engaged the moral attention, forming a habit of mind. And such habits of mind, because they come down to us without mere reference to pain-pleasure criteria, are of a character that qualifies as moral-theological, entitling us to say that we feel it somehow sinful to transgress on what one might call "two commandments"—namely, "Thou shalt not discriminate against someone because he is Jewish"; and "Thou shalt not heedlessly exploit nature."

Sinful Conduct

The *capacity* to recognize particular habits of conduct as sinful continues to reside in us. Non-Christians, and even atheists, are for the most part prepared to acknowledge that, however it was that they came to reach certain moral decisions, most people are, in fact, potential clients of argumentation that is extra-instrumentally moral. For instance, thoughtful folk will ponder the moral question whether a fetus is a human being,

an intellectual acknowledgment of which would obviously overwhelm utilitarian arguments having to do with the sovereignty
of maternal inclinations.

What is the principal source of these moral distinctions,
if not the Bible? One wonders then about the desuetude of the
word *sin*. It is as infrequently heard outside our churches as
the word *God*. And, of course, the terms tend to be associated.

The three generic sanctions that cause societies to cohere
are social, legal, and divine. It is not hard to come up with
examples of a deed that offends one of the sanctions, but not
the other two. One could arrive tieless at a black-tie party
without arousing the police or, one supposes, divine displea-
sure. One can (illegally) transport a bottle of whiskey from
Connecticut to New York without affronting one's neighbors
or one's God. And one can take in vain the name of the Lord
without incurring civil or social disapproval. On the other hand,
the three sanctions often make common cause. Murder, rape,
theft are only the most obvious examples.

The question before the house, however, has to do with
that category of offenses against which social and even legal
sanctions are atrophying. In most municipalities one can smoke
marijuana with *de facto* legal impunity. And in most middle-
and upper-class ("progressive") households, the weed is
smoked with scant social opprobrium. The use of marijuana is
not (to my knowledge) specifically proscribed by Judeo-
Christianity. But this is so, one supposes, only because no
episcopal authority of note has got around to the particulariza-
tion of the generic law against gluttony. It reasonably follows
that to dope the mind is in the same category of excess as to
overstuff the body and is, therefore, a deadly sin.

What would happen if religious sanctions against the use
of marijuana were made explicit? Would we notice any difference? When Dr. Rosenthal talks about vitalizing an ethos
against the use of marijuana—a sanction made explicit by
declining to tolerate young junkies coming to your house to
smoke there—he does not mean that our ministers, rabbis, and
priests, inveighing against drug taking, will suddenly breathe

life into a social sanction, much as the sanction against throwing refuse into the water was vivified by the work of Rachel Carson and those others of the natural ministry who made us conscious of the tenderness of the planet. If the Pope, speaking *ex cathedra*, were to declare sinful the use of marijuana, the use of the drug by Catholics would diminish. But in general, an effective ethos needs nowadays to be engineered by extra-theological persuasion.

Whatever became of sin?

The highly touted playboy philosophy is ever so much in point here. Some years ago the chaplain to Yale University, the Rev. William Sloane Coffin, was asked to comment on the (rampantly) free sex that characterized the Woodstock generation. The Rev. Coffin would rather have bombed the dikes in North Vietnam than answer the question by saying that the Judeo-Christian code specifies monogamy as proper sexual behavior—sexual behavior which is "right" as distinguished from sexual behavior which is "wrong." Rather, Dr. Coffin said that anything—anything—can be overdone. For instance (he explained), drinking a beer won't hurt you, but you have got to guard against becoming an alcoholic. The conclusion that was supposed to be derived from this, one supposes, was that a Yale student should not have more than one concubine at a time, because out there in the murky psychological world of sex, there is the equivalent of alcoholism—alcoholism of the senses. Take too many lovers or mistresses and you deprive sex of its sublimer meaning, much as, if you chug-a-lug a bottle of Mouton Rothschild 1959, you dilute the pleasure of it. The Reverend had, of course, some very good points here, psychological, sociological, and even biological: but the way in which he made them reminded us of the lengths some people go, even if they are formal ministers of God, to guard against the invocation of sin, and therefore recognition of the authoritative source where sin is defined.

I remember about the same time reading a letter by a young groupie in *Rolling Stone* magazine. "What I worry about is," she said in her published letter to the editor, "is semen fattening?" If it is, the Rev. Mr. Coffin would have been able to buttress his argument against promiscuous sexuality with another empirical argument without running the danger of using the word *sin*.

In his essay on "sin" in the Great Books' *Syntopicon*, Mortimer Adler gives us this conspectus:

> In the pagan and Judaeo-Christian conceptions of sin, the fundamental meaning seems to depend upon the relation of man to the gods or to God, whether that itself be considered in terms of law or love. The vicious act may be conceived as one which is contrary to nature or reason. The criminal act may be conceived as a violation of the law of man, injurious to the welfare of the state or to its members. Both may involve the notions of responsibility and fault. Both may involve evil and wrongdoing. But unless the act transgresses the law of God, it is not sinful. The divine law which is transgressed may be the natural law that God instills in human reason. But the act is sinful if the person who commits the act turns away from God to the worship or love of other things.[1]

Loss of Divine Sanctions

So then: How is a society that strives for virtuous conduct going to encourage right-minded institutions and right-minded behavior without invoking the divine sanction? Those who despair of the final secularization of our society should note that the word *sin* survives when used as a metaphor. It is a sign of latent life in the word that, reaching for final gravity with which to denounce or to describe a particular situation, one hears such things as "John's treatment of Jane was really . . . sinful." We are here suggesting that behavior ultimately offensive is properly described not merely as "illegal" or "antisocial," but, verily, as opposed to the laws of God himself.

And then, too, the idea of expiation is not entirely foreign to our culture. In formal religious circumstances Catholics go to confession. There they enumerate their sins, plead contrition, and receive a "penance" and contingent forgiveness. Judges in criminal law, under pressure to lighten the prison load and to mete out more imaginative punishments than time in jail, have recently cocked their ears to listen to the recommendations of Prison Fellowship and have shown signs of inventiveness—one hundred hours of community service, that kind of thing. Perhaps one day, not far off, a judge will give a young man caught defacing a synagogue or a church, as an alternative to the statutorily permissible one year in jail, an assignment of a half-dozen books of holy literature to study, from which it would be hoped that the meaning of his desecration would dawn on him. That would be an example of the secular law reaching out to reinforce the divine law.

What happened along the way was the alienation of the secular culture from the biblical culture. Irving Kristol has written that the most important *political* development of the nineteenth century was the wholesale loss of religious faith, the implication of which is that man's natural idealism should turn to utopianism, which always boils down to ideology. Enter the Twentieth Century.

The loss of religious sanctions imposes on the remaining sanctions a heavier weight than they are designed to handle. And when that happens and society gets serious about something, it has recourse only to force. Nelson Rockefeller's solution to the drug problem was to take a drug user, put him in jail and throw away the keys. The great totalitarian triumvirate—Hitler, Stalin, Mao—took the legal sanction further than Cotton Mather took hellfire. Or put another way, in imposing their sanctions, Hitler, Stalin, and Mao brought us hell on earth. And elsewhere, Kristol touched a grace note of piquancy wonderfully, awesomely grave in its implications. As far as he could figure out, he said, in New York City, a man could have sexual intercourse with an eighteen-year-old girl on a public stage, just so long as she was being paid the minimum wage. And in Sweden, a father can be jailed for spanking his son but not for sleeping with his daughter.

Social sanctions against disgusting behavior? (*Disgusting*? What's that? "When one asks how a sense of guilt arises in anyone, one is told something one cannot dispute: people feel guilty. Pious people call it sinful when they have done something they know to be 'bad.' But then one sees how little this answer tells one," so wrote Sigmund Freud.) Though by no means all sanctions should be made into law, it is true that sanctions tend to lose vigor if uncodified. And even then, they lose vigor if the ethos that supports the laws is attenuated. Legal constraints surrender, up against the force of massive contumacy. As well, at this point, stop the spread of pornography in America as, during prohibition, one could hope to stop the use of liquor.

Sin sits in the back of the bus. But it is still there, a presence in the conscience. And this is so probably because it was so intended by the First Mover—that man, *in pluribus*, should harbor the capacity to distinguish between right and wrong, and that he should feel something between an itch and a compulsion to exercise that capacity.

An example: There is a famine in the land, and you harbor a supply of grain. But you harbor, also, a secret. You happen to know that a caravan of supplies is on its way and will arrive within a few days. Can you charge for your supply of grain a very high price, as if it alone stood between your clients and starvation? Yes, you are at liberty to do so, St. Thomas Aquinas said; but it would be wrong. *Wrong*? Why? Because it is *wrong*, sinful; *Ipse res loquitur*! And you shouldn't need Immanuel Kant to explain it to you.

I said over the air a while back that I believed in metaphysical equality, that otherwise there was *no way* I could be made to believe that Mother Teresa and Sister Boom Boom were equal. I had a letter from someone who said he does not understand, and that he cannot find in any dictionary authority to use the word *metaphysical* to define in any intelligible way the word *equality*. Why (I wrote him), it means here *equal in the eyes of God* and that is all the explanation *I* need: equal beyond measurement. I find it sinful to reason otherwise about Sister Boom Boom.

It isn't only Christian clergymen who speak of the necessity of a spiritual revival in order to forward civilized life. Years ago Professor Richard Weaver pointed out what should be obvious, namely that Marxism and Communism are redemptive creeds, while liberalism has no eschatology, no ultimate sense of consummation. Lacking that, it is at a grave disadvantage contending with secular religions which offer the vision of comprehensive achievements to their flock.

The rediscovery of sin, as defined in the Bible, would cause us to look up and note the infinite horizons that beckon us toward better conduct, better lives, nobler visions.

Wrong Use of the Bible

But it is neither charitable nor just to assign all of the blame to secular forces. The diminished Bible, in our culture, is in part owing to diminished faith and derivative hostility. But it is also owing, in part, to opportunistic uses of the Bible by those who wish to see in it authority to ply their special positions in world politics. The attempt to transform the Bible into a mandate for socialism is widely recognized, but I think less of that mutilation than of another. I have been vexed by conclusions arrived at by the National Council of Churches and by the Catholic bishops during recent years concerning our nuclear deterrent. Its primary assertions focus on the innocents who necessarily perish in any hypothetical nuclear engagement.

Let us take that problem on.

Dmitri and Valerian are twin brothers. Both are interested in the arts, particularly in ballet. They turn eighteen, and Valerian fails his physical—he has a disqualifying heart murmur. Dmitri, however, is drafted and in due course finds himself attached to a missile silo battery. His brother Valerian, mean-while, goes to the ballet at night but during the day works at a factory that manufactures missiles. Dmitri, in standing by the trigger of his SS-18, is doing what he is told to do. Valerian, standing by the assembly line, pouring whatever it is you pour into missiles to enable them to destroy Paris and Detroit, is doing what *he* is told to do.

Some people, at this point, are willing to give you earnest money on their flexibility. We will concede, they say, that missile factories fall under roughly the same category as missile launchers. Therefore, it is morally acceptable to include Vale-rian's factory as a counterforce target. But the organic porosity of that factory tends to overwhelm the search for logical moral boundaries. You see, Valerian's cousin Nikita is engaged in mining the special metals required to manufacture that mortal missile. He works out there in the Urals. And, in fact, as recently as last year, he got a medal, along with his co-workers, in acknowledgment of the national dependence of the Union of Soviet Socialist Republics on his work.

I do not need to draw it out to show that the exercise I have done involving Nikita can as easily be done to demonstrate the dependence of the front line soldier on the farmer who grows the wheat, without which Nikita, the miner, could not continue to forward to Valerian, the missile-maker, the metals necessary to forward to Dmitri the finished missiles that aim at Paris and Detroit. It may be that the next war, if there is to be another war, God forbid, will be over, so to speak, after a single volley, rendering subsequent support from the farmers to Nikita, from Nikita to Valerian, and from Valerian to Dmitri a routine logistical problem, transacted without the umbilical urgency of war-making (the assumption here is that the enemy was disposed of in a first strike). But, of course, that might not happen. The missile silo—or its sister silo—may be needed again. And, of course, if the war goes forward with tactical weapons, all the farmers and all the Nikitas and all the Valerians will be working day and night, causing the moralists to chew their nails over the question: Are these, indeed, innocent parties?

From all of this, and much derivative reasoning, I emerge doubting the relevance of neo-Christian moral pedagogy based on traditional distinctions that have sought to discriminate, for a relatively short period in history (remember that during the Middle Ages, the siege of whole towns was the convention; and in the Old Testament, entire regions were made to suffer for the sins of the few) between the guilty and the innocent, the activists and the bystanders, the combatants and the non-combatants, I ask then: Does the proposition that it is no longer possible morally to distinguish between the military and the civilian populations in any way help us to advance our strategic thinking along moral lines? I think it does; but, in between, it becomes necessary to linger over a second proposition.

It is that the most important endeavor of man is to seek to distinguish between right and wrong. Hardly a new proposition; but one which, in my judgment, we tend to affirm without a secure sense of what it is that we value more, and should do so, and what less. My proposition is that the love of life is a holy sanctified impulse, while the veneration of life is idolatry.

Many people today are beginning, as I see it, to slur the distinction between loving life and venerating it. To love life is wholesome; to venerate it is, surely, to violate the First Commandment, which permits the veneration only of God. To venerate life is to attach to it first importance. Surely if we were all to do that, any talk of war, just or unjust, prudent or imprudent, limited or unlimited, provoked or unprovoked, would be an exercise in moral atavism, it having been decided that the taking of life, because life is venerated, was a comprehensively prohibited act.

If we love life, then we are forced to ask: *Why* do we love it? To answer merely by giving biological explanations—for instance, that sensual pleasures ensue on breathing when suffocation threatens, or eating when one is hungry, resting when one is weary, voiding when the stomach is cramped—is morally uncivilized. That is to say, it is to give answers that are incomplete, for those who understand man as more merely than a biological composition.

We cherish life mostly because it permits us to love, and to be loved. And we cherish it in a dimension wholly other from that which gives leisure by satisfying biological appetites. We love life because there is a range of experience given to us in life that regularly pleases, sometimes excites, occasionally elates. I have mentioned, preeminently, the joys of loving and being loved, and there are the delights captured by poetry and music. But all these are overwhelmed by God.

So it is, at this point, that I intrude the distinction between love and veneration. We venerate him, we love one another. It is my suspicion that the evolution of the idea of selective conscientious objection to the draft, that the opposition of aid to those contending against Communism—whether in Angola or Afghanistan or Nicaragua—is, whatever its sophisticated rationale, really a part of a movement toward the veneration of life, such that all other considerations are as quickly subordinated as a computer nowadays reorders all derivative calculations, once you have altered the value of the prime number. I think that that is the direction mistakenly in which many of our Christian moralists are headed. To help themselves, they begin by making false assumptions—such as those that distinguish, or rather seek to do so, between combatant and noncombatant members of an aggressive community. Then they find themselves speaking about prudent and imprudent uses of deterrent weapons. And, finally, we have the sense—or, at least, some of us do—that what is going on is a creeping philosophical reconciliation with that definition of life that does not stop short—ask Bukovsky, ask Mendeleev, ask Solzhenitsyn, ask Shcharansky, ask Sakharov—that does not stop short of transforming life, the life we properly love, into mere biological life. And when, the challenge having confronted us, we prefer mere biological survival over the mere *risk* of death in pursuit of Christian life, we come perilously close to worshiping false gods. Or so it would appear to me.

A Kingdom Not of This World

It is most awfully strange for a man of my age, approaching senior citizenship, born to Christian parents who loved God, each other, and their ten children, with joy, with curiosity, with respect, to find myself after three-quarters of a lifetime in the faith almost everywhere assaulted by arguments emanating alike from agnostics, Christian laymen and churchmen of all faiths, that seem to pay in some cases, most literally, no attention whatever to Christian teaching which speaks of the end of the world quite fatalistically—or where attention is given to apocalypse—to speak of it with a kind of mythological detachment that characterizes quaint literary references to Eve and the serpent, or Jonah and the whale.

No biblical paradox can be more relevant today than Christ's, which said that his Kingdom is not of this world. As a child, I simply interpreted this as meaning that Christ had a different address from our own, and perhaps could be reached only by air mail. As a young man, I interpreted this as an injunction to care especially about Christlike things, rather than about things of this world. But in due course, I smelled Manichaeism in this, which a natural hedonism helped me to overcome. As an older man, though perhaps one who has yet to reach full maturity, I understand Christ to have told us that although his Kingdom was not of this world, his is a Kingdom he will one day, let us pray, share with us—leaving it to us, while inhabiting our own city, to be counseled by the lessons Christ taught us, and inspired by the example he set of his love for us; by coming to us. It can never be suspected of the Man who died on the cross that he venerated the life which, to be sure, he loved. Does this reduce to strategic formulae? Only negatively. It hardly instructs us to be enthusiastic about, or to deplore, the INF Treaty, announced recently. But yes, I would resist any philosophical usurpation that sought to put biological life on the throne. No, I do not deduce from this any concrete arrangements for facing the most awful threat of this century, animated by a fetid materialism. But I would deduce this much, namely that any deceits we practice, for instance in inviting the disability of our deterrent powers by seeking to distinguish between combatant and noncombatant; that any stratagems we follow ostensibly in pursuit of morality, when what we are really pursuing is false idols, do not become a country as blessed as our own has been.

The profoundest commitments we make as a nation are based on our sense of the religious dimension in life. The very idea of sacrifice for the common good is biblical in its provenance. We look to the fountainhead of truth and wisdom, to the Book in which the story is told of the rise and fall of nations, reminding us that just as our future is in the hands of the Lord, so is it in the hands of the Lord whether our country will seek to requite the blessings he has showered on us.

Chapter 2, Notes

1. Mortimer J. Adler, "Sin" in *The Great Ideas: A Syntopicon of Great Books of the Western World* (Chicago: Encyclopedia Britannica, 1952), 2:756.

PART 2

FORMING A
CHRISTIAN MIND

Chapter 3

The Christian and Society

Os Guinness

*H*ave you ever been in eastern Europe and visited one of those countries where the militiamen go around in threes? The reason for it, it is said, is that the first of the three is the one who knows how to read, the second the one who knows how to write, and the third is there to keep an eye on those other two dangerous intellectuals.

Many churches make one feel like that, I'm afraid. Speak intelligently for more than two minutes and with more than one thought in each, and you are considered dangerously intellectual and unspiritual. Part of what I appreciated about Congress on the Bible II was its seriousness, its evident desire to tackle the big issues in light of the Word and our world today. And they are big issues, and tough, too. So we need to forswear simple answers, be prepared to pray, think and sweat intellectually in order to see where we are today and what the Lord would have us do.

Let me open up this momentous theme of "the Christian and Society" or, as I prefer, "Church and Society" with a story and a quotation. Soviet leader Nikita Khrushchev used to tell of a time when there was a wave of petty theft in the U.S.S.R., and the authorities put guards at the factories. At one of the timberworks in Leningrad the guard knew the workers well. The first evening, out came Pyotr Petrovich with a wheelbarrow and, on the wheelbarrow, a great bulky sack with a suspicious-looking object inside.

"Come on, Petrovich," said the guard. "What have you got there?"

"Just sawdust and shavings," Petrovich replied.

"Come on," the guard said, "I wasn't born yesterday. Tip it out." Out it came—nothing but sawdust and shavings. So he was allowed to put it all back again and go home.

The same thing happened every night all week, and the guard was getting extremely frustrated. Finally, his curiosity overcame his frustration.

"Petrovich," he said, "I know you. Tell me what you're smuggling out of here, and I'll let you go."

"Wheelbarrows," said Petrovich.

We may laugh, but remember that in the arena of church and society the laugh is on us as evangelicals. We have set up patrols to check for secularism around the country, but the devil has trundled secularization right past our eyes into the church. We have conducted spot checks, looking for any conceivable lapse in biblical authority, but the devil has trundled anarchy right into our lifestyles—past the front doors of our homes.

Back in the early seventies, a professor at Oxford turned to me, knowing I was a Christian, and said, "By the end of the seventies, who will be the worldliest Christians in America?" I must have looked a bit puzzled, and he went on, "I guarantee it will be the fundamentalists."

At the time that seemed startling. Worldliest? Fundamentalists then were world-denying by definition. But in 1987, after a year of Christian scandal and shame, we hardly need to pause at that question. One of the deepest reasons behind the corruption of evangelicalism and fundamentalism is a profound inadequacy in understanding how the church should engage society.

Now the quotation. One hundred years ago, the German philosopher Friedrich Nietzsche made the remark that when God dies, culture becomes "weightless." When I first read that, I was deeply moved for three reasons.

First, weightlessness is a powerful biblical theme. It is the precise opposite of glory. The glory of God is far more than his renown or radiance. Glory is God's own inexpressible reality, a reality so real that it alone has gravity and weight— the only "really real reality" in the entire universe. Therefore, when things move away from God, they become hollow and weightless, and we can accurately say, "Ichabod" ("The glory has departed") or, "Mene, mene, tekel, upharsin" ("You are weighed in the balance and found weightless or wanting"). That is why idols, by contrast with God, are literally "nothings." That is why revival is the refilling of a nation with "the knowledge of the glory of the LORD, as the waters cover the sea" (Habakkuk 2:14).

Second, Nietzsche was addressing his remarks to England, my homeland, at a time when most things appeared well both for the church and the nation. But Nietzsche had looked below the surface and had seen the hollowing out that had begun. A generation characterized by "convictions" had been followed by one of "conventions" and was soon to be followed by one of "addictions." National greatness was, in fact, being hollowed out before World War I dealt it an irrecoverable blow. England was growing weightless from the inside.

Third, many observers say that the 1980s are America's weightless years—a second gilded age. True, Walt Whitman spoke of American hollowness a century ago, but for obvious reasons the process was arrested. However, in the Reagan years, at point after point, there has been a growing sense of weightlessness, of loss of reality, of loss of the real stuff that will keep a nation great. Again, the church shows many of the same signs of weightlessness we see in the world. And one of the basic reasons is a lack of engagement in society in ways that are spiritually realistic as well as socially relevant.

In sum, church and society is not just a large, abstract

topic. It is not even just one key topic among many. It is the test bed that reveals the character and health of all our truths. If we do not demonstrate them in the crucible of society, we can take it that they mean nothing, whatever we profess. In other words, this is far more than a topic for the "socially aware" or the "spiritually concerned." Get to grips with this topic and we get to grips with all the deep questions of worship and discipleship in the modern world.

Let me lay out what I think are six foundation considerations that we need today as we engage as God's people in our society. I want to outline these considerations as pairs of ideas. You will note that the halves of each pair are not only closely connected but are interdependent.

Two Perspectives

All engagement in society requires or reveals an answer to the question: How do we see society? There is a tendency for us to oscillate from one viewpoint to another—one moment optimistic, the next pessimistic, or whatever. But the view of society we find in the Scriptures is a bifocal vision. Always and everywhere at once, society is two things: God's gift to us, and the devil's gauntlet thrown down before us, to challenge us to worship him and not Christ.

On the one hand, *society is God's gift to us*. To be sure, in comparison with what it might have been if there had been no Fall and what it will be when Christ comes again, what we see today is marred by evil, filled with pain and ruined with brokenness. Yet even when we have looked at evil full-faced, we still know that society is God's gift. God is as decisive in sustaining society as society is decisive in shaping us. Only when we remember the former do we prevent the latter from becoming a fatalism that unnerves us.

Many Christians have forgotten both these truths, and modern individualism is a big reason why. Sin has always pivoted on the claim to the right to oneself, along with the accompanying claim to the right to see things from one's own point of view. Modern individualism, therefore, bolsters the pretense that we do not need others in any profound way.

But as biblical people, we should know that individualism is a dangerous illusion. We are social people willy-nilly. We are who we are because we have grown up face to face. We live, work, and play side by side. It is, therefore, very important to us that God decisively sustains the world that decisively shapes us. Despite its fallenness, society is still God's gift to us, and we should be thankful.

On the other hand, *society is also the devil's gauntlet*. However much we experience in it of wonder, love and joy, society is under an alien rule. Society is part of the first of the big trio—the world, the flesh, and the devil. Thus, however much it is God's gift, society also contains a spirit, a system and a structure that stand over against the kingdom of God and his Christ.

Yes, the devil failed once. Out there in the desert, he promised everything. But God's great advocate overcame God's great adversary, and the devil left the field licked.

Still the devil knows that where he failed with the Master, he may succeed with the servants. So he comes to us, and he invites us to enter and enjoy society at every level—from our work to our play, from the humblest levels up to the boardrooms of the country. "All this is yours," he says, "if only . . ." And buried in this invitation are the questions: Who is Lord? and Have we faced up to the nature of the system?

"Pick it up," says the evil one. "All is yours . . . if you worship me."

Society, in other words, is the devil's gauntlet thrown down before us. But that is not because we are the innocents and the world is tempting. Rather, we are the temptable ones. The world is simply our hearts writ large. Our hearts are simply the world writ small. So our view of society needs to be deeply realistic. If society is God's gift to us, it is also the devil's gauntlet, and that bifocal vision should shape our perspective.

Two Principles

After the question, How do we see the world? comes a second one, How do we act in the world? Two great master principles have characterized the church at its most penetrating. The first is the *Protagonist principle* which flows from the theme "Christ *over* all" and has as its key word, *total*.

The story of the exodus provides an Old Testament example. The whole issue with pharaoh was lordship. He who can liberate is he who is lord. As the bargaining went on, pharaoh relented enough to let the Israelite men go, at least for worship. Moses said, No. "Let my people go" meant not just the men and not just for worship. Men, women, and children must go, and for good. Then a remarkable little phrase is added: "Not a hoof is to be left behind" (Exodus 10:26).

A New Testament example can be found in Luke 5. Peter, as a fisherman, was glad to allow Jesus to preach from his boat. But Jesus said to Peter, "Put out into deep water, and let down the nets for a catch" (v. 4).

We can almost hear Peter reply. "Look, Lord, I'll listen to you as my teacher all day long, but when it comes to fishing, that's my job."

We know the result. Peter found that Jesus was Lord of nature, too, and he could only respond, "Go away from me, Lord; I am a sinful man!" (v. 8). Christ was Lord of nature as well as truth. He is the Alpha and the Omega. He is the source, guide, and goal of all there is. That is why every eye will one day see him, every tongue will be stopped, and every knee will bow. After all, as Abraham Kuyper said, expressing the protagonist principle perfectly, "There is not an inch of any sphere of life of which Jesus Christ the Lord does not say, 'Mine.'"

The second principle is the *Antagonist principle*. It flows from the theme "Christ *over against* all that which does not bow to him," and the key word is *tension*. The Lord himself puts the point unmistakably in Exodus 20: "I am the LORD your God. . . . You shall have no other gods before [to set against] me" (vv. 2, 3). Over forty times in Leviticus 18 and the following chapters, there is the recurring assertion, "I am the LORD." Each time it accompanies a strict instruction not to do as the Egyptians or the Canaanites did, neither following their idols nor copying their ideas and institutions.

The reason? The Lord is the jealous one, the one who brooks no rivals. Since he is our "decisive Other," he demands of us a decisive contrast with everything that is over against him and his ways. Most wonderful of all, the deepest reason is not puritanical but personal. It is "that you may belong to me."

In short, God and the world stand crosswise. We are in the world but not of it. To be faithful to him we have to be foreign to the world. We are not to be conformed but transformed by the renewing of our minds.

Of course, the Protagonist principle and the Antagonist principle must never be separated. They go hand in hand. Without the former, the latter would create a "we/they" division. The Protagonist principle means there is no hatred of the world or false asceticism here. Yes, the world is passing away, and we are passing through the world. But in the memorable phrase of Peter Berger, we are only "against the world for the world."

Two Deficiencies

The third foundation consideration grows from the question: Where has our engagement with the world gone wrong? Here we have to face the fact that under the conditions of the modern world, or what is called "modernity," a key breakdown between faith and obedience has occurred, one which is proving lethal to Christian integrity and effectiveness.

The full explanation of this breakdown is complicated. Its roots are not only theological, but philosophical, sociological and spiritual. As a result of a combination of many things, two glaring deficiencies in our discipleship have grown common.

First, as modern followers of Christ, we face a peculiar

temptation *to break the link between belief and behavior*. Anyone who wants to observe religion in the modern world and find the sort of belief that behaves would be advised to look at the cults rather than at Christians. What cult members believe may be bizarre and the way they behave even worse, but to their credit, there is a consistency between their belief and behavior which is rare in today's world.

Some years ago, the Queen of the Belgians was visiting Poland. She went to mass one day, accompanied by a party official. Noticing that he seemed to know a lot about the Catholic liturgy, she turned to him and asked, "Are you a Catholic?"

The official, looking embarrassed, replied, "Believing, Madam. Not practicing, I'm afraid."

"Oh, of course," she said, "you must be a Communist."

He said, "Practicing, not believing, I'm afraid."

In other words, the breakdown between belief and behavior is not only an evangelical or even a Christian problem. It has affected almost all beliefs, though it hits us harder as Christians because of our specially strong claims as to what faith means.

There has been considerable discussion recently about "cafeteria Catholicism"—mix your own morals, choose your own church, pick your own preference, and so on. ("Yes, we love the Pope, but we don't follow his teaching.") But if there is a "cafeteria Catholicism," there is equally an "easy-care evangelicalism," and both are a result of the breakdown between believing and behaving.

A simple example is popular evangelical theology—some of the sloppiest and most superficial sentiment that has ever passed for theology. I cited an incident in *The Gravedigger File* that many people thought I had made up. In fact, it was true. I just had not used the name of the person.

Some years ago, I watched a few minutes of a program on the electronic church. A black singer sang an old spiritual in a way which threatened to inject reality into the proceedings. The show's hostess clapped her hands, rolled her eyes heavenward and cooed, "Fantastic, brother! Fantastic! Christianity is so fantastic! Who cares whether or not it's true!"

That incident was a few years ago, and many readers took it as purely funny. But after the scandalous revelations of 1987, the consequences of such corrupt theology in the lives of Jim and Tammy Faye Bakker have proved to be no joke.

Milder everyday examples are common. Not long ago, the call to worship in our church, a leading center of Episcopalian renewal, went like this: "Come with me, walk with me, run with me, fly with me. We will roam the Father's land together. . . . Feeling the warmth of the sun about, we will know the loveliness of every hour." I was in one of Washington's leading evangelical Presbyterian churches which had as its confession, "Father, forgive us, for we have not lived up to our dreams." From the Hallmark card theology of a thousand churches to the nauseating nonsense of PTL, American evangelicalism is awash in a sloppy, sentimental, superficial theology that wouldn't power a clockwork mouse, let alone a disciple of Christ in our tough modern world.

The second deficiency in discipleship concerns *the broken link between the private world and the public world*, through which faith becomes "privately engaging, but socially irrelevant."

The clearest example I know came during a *New York Times* interview with a celebrated business leader who was also a Christian. Asked what he believed in, he replied, "I believe in God, the family, and McDonalds hamburgers. And when I get to the office, I reverse the order."

Let us hope he was being facetious in a manner not picked up in the printed interview. But even if he was, he was only saying what millions of Christians do every single day without realizing it. Their faith flourishes at home, at church, in prayer breakfasts before work, or in the Bible study group during the lunch hour. But work itself is a different world, with a different way of doing things. Without realizing it, millions of Christians hang their faith, along with their hats and coats, at the door.

The link between the private world of faith and the public world of work is severed.

It is true that there are magnificent exceptions to this problem. It is also true that both these deficiencies are offset by reactions that head in the opposite direction. For example, if one general problem in the church is *permissiveness* ("anything goes"), some Christians have veered to the opposite extreme—a new kind of *particularism*. They see one way as the only Christian way of doing things—with the added insult that if you do not do it that way, you must not be a Christian.

Or again, if one general problem is the *privatization* of faith, some Christians have recently swung to the other extreme—*politicization*. They act as if politics in general and Washington in particular are the be-all and end-all of Christian obedience.

Both these errors, particularism and politicization, are a dangerous trap for disciples. But it is still the case that the opposite problems—permissiveness and not particularism, privatization and not politicization—are greater for evangelicalism as a whole.

Dostoevsky's celebrated saying, "When God is dead, everything is permitted," could in America be equally well translated, "When God is dead, nothing is owed." For a characteristic of modern America is the absence of obligation. We owe nothing to anyone, except to ourselves. Words mean little and bind no one. Therefore, a deep danger of evangelicalism is that, even as we trumpet our concern for biblical authority, we reveal the disappearance of the Bible's "binding address." The Scriptures still address us in general but no longer bind us to anything in particular.

Two Reminders

The fourth pair of founding considerations grows from the question: What is the setting in which we are discussing these questions? Clearly we are not raising these questions in a vacuum or in a purely academic setting. Nor are we living in a great age of faith, such as the times of the Reformation or the first Great Awakening. Our cultural situation adds an urgent reminder to this whole discussion at two points. On the one hand, the nation is at a turning point, principally because of *the decreasing influence of faith on society*. On the other hand, the church is at a turning point, principally because of *an increasing influence of society on faith* .

I have a hunch that the year 1986 is going to turn out to be the ironic parallel for conservatives of the year 1968 for liberals. You may remember that in 1968, liberals hailed victory. For the first time, there was a solid majority against the Vietnam war. In fact, they were right: the majority was against the war. But it was also against liberals. It was Nixon's "emerging new majority." Thus, 1968 was both the high point and a turning point, after which the tide turned and flowed relentlessly against them.

The year 1986 may prove to be the same for conservatives. The Statue of Liberty celebrations in July saw the high tide of the claims for the conservative revolution. Now, less than two years later, most of those claims are in tatters. The conservative counterrevolution, like the liberal revolution before it, has been betrayed by its illusions and inner contradictions.

This means that the period we are entering is one of decisive reckoning because the United States is approaching the close of a generation-long crisis of cultural authority. After the great 1960s lurch in directions liberal, radical, and secular came the great 1980s counterlurch in directions conservative, traditional, and religious. Now, with the failure of both revolutions on their own terms, we enter the showdown years that will reveal which faiths, which world views, and which moral principles are going to prove decisive in shaping the nation over the next generations. The nation is at a turning point because of a decreasing influence of faith.

But we can see equally plainly that the church is at a turning point because of an increasing influence of culture. Americans used to speak much of their "exceptionalism." Today there is only one place left where America is still exceptional—the strength of religion. In a world in which modernity and secularity seem to go hand in hand, the United States is simultaneously the most modern and the most religious of modern countries. Yet with the shrinking discrepancy between indicators (church attendance, giving, praying, and so on) and the social influence—the former up and the latter down—the exception cannot continue for long. There is too little religion and too much religiosity in the church. The church's showdown period is beginning, too, when its true integrity and effectiveness will be revealed.

Two Requirements before the World

The fifth pair of founding considerations are an answer to the question: What do we most need as we engage with our society? I am sure we might each put forward our own short list. Let me suggest two things that relate to our public witness—the need for *a Christian mind* and *a public philosophy*.

In 1976, the year *Newsweek* called the "Year of the Evangelical," many observers asked whether the evangelical community would make the impact which its history, numbers, and opportunity might lead one to expect. The answer was generally, No. The main reason given was that evangelicals were unlikely to think in any distinctively Christian way.

Such predictions have proved lamentably correct. Failure to "think Christianly" is the Achilles heel of English-speaking evangelicalism. While the Puritans were magnificently different, evangelicals since the Great Awakening have by and large displayed only a "ghost mind," hollowed out by various forces, which for all their spiritual passion led toward a general anti-intellectualism. Since then, with exceptions only proving the rule, there has been no powerful evangelical mind. Thus, at most of the decisive moments in American thinking—Emerson's "intellectual Declaration of Independence" at Harvard in 1837, the rise of higher education and of liberalism, and so on— evangelicals were not so much out-thought as out of it. They still are today.

When will we face the fact that our deep-rooted anti-intellectualism is worse than ineffective? It is sub-Christian, disobedient, anti-spiritual, and unloving, and only when we root out the last traces of it can we hope to exercise the public influence that faithfulness to Christ demands. In the end, thinking Christianly has nothing to do with being intellectual. God forbid. It is a matter of faithfulness and loving God.

Let me be specific. Since living in Washington the past three years, the spiritual lesson that I have benefited from most is the reminder of our grand priority: that above all else we are to love the Lord our God with all our heart, soul, strength, and mind. Christ himself and not "Christianity" is our first love, our primary call, our fundamental loyalty.

I confess that I needed that reminder, and I have benefited from adjusting to that priority. I thank God for it. But to be candid, I am saddened by the selectiveness of what it means around Washington. There are too many who love the Lord with all their hearts, souls, and strength but who leave their "minds" off the list. Under the guise of an ostensibly spiritual priority, they rationalize the disobedience of anti-intellectualism. Unless this generation of evangelicals confronts its centuries old habit of anti-intellectualism, we do not have the slightest chance of penetrating modern society for Christ.

The second external requirement is *a contribution to America's public philosophy* that has both Christian integrity and public credibility. The United States has always been characterized by its astonishing blend of liberty, diversity, and harmony. Put differently, consensus-building has become one of America's greatest achievements and special needs. Despite such diversity, consensus maintains unity. Despite change, it maintains continuity, and it is this common vision of the common good that Walter Lippman called the "public philosophy."

Obviously, a key part of this public philosophy has been an agreed understanding of the place of religion in public life, and of the guiding principles within which citizens with religious differences can contend with each other in the public sphere. But equally obviously, if the public philosophy is in poor shape today, this particular part is in chronic disrepair.

Look at the controversies over religion-and-politics in the last ten years. Debates have been fruitlessly polarized, issues dominated by the extremes. Resolution has been sought reflexively from the courts. The two religion clauses have been pitted against each other, and there has been an evident breakdown of any shared understanding of how religiously-grounded differences should be negotiated in the public sphere. Worst of all, evangelicals and fundamentalists have often made the problems worse. With their better voices unheard and those heard relying solely on a confrontational style concerned solely with "me/my/our" interests, they, too, have caused great damage to the public philosophy.

We need to be heard to say, "Christian justice is not justice for Christians. It is justice for everybody." Rights are universal and responsibilities mutual. So a right for one is a right for another and a responsibility for both. A right for a Protestant is a right for a Catholic, is a right for a Jew, is a right for a Humanist, is a right for a Mormon, and a right for the believer of any faith under God's wide heaven.

The First Amendment in this sense is the epitome of public justice and serves as the Golden Rule for civic life: rights are best protected and responsibilities best exercised if we guard for others the rights we would wish guarded for ourselves.

Beyond the principled reasons for a public philosophy are pragmatic ones. The recent contentious debates, at least in their high-octane form, are not likely to continue forever. "War weariness" is already setting in. The public is tired of the trench warfare over religion and public life. But if we are not careful, the danger is of a great sea change in public attitudes. Instead of faith and freedom being viewed as blood brothers, as they have been for two hundred years, they will come to be viewed as in opposing corners—with titanic implications for the gospel and the nation.

Two Requirements before the Lord

The last pair of founding considerations concern two requirements that we need before the Lord. If we ask what it is we most need, the answer in two words is: God himself. But let me just draw out two simple requirements that need stressing because they are so simple that we easily overlook them—a proclamation of the Word and a visitation of the Spirit.

President Lyndon Johnson used to tell a story of a preacher who prepared a stirring but rather complicated sermon that required notes. On his way to church he dropped the notes, and they were eaten by a dog. Unabashed, he climbed into the pulpit and said, "Brothers and sisters, I'm afraid a dog ate my sermon notes on the way to church. I'm just going to have to rely on what the Holy Spirit tells me, but I promise I'll do better next week."

That may be closer to the situation in many American pulpits than we realize. Having visited almost all the countries in the English-speaking world, I would say that I know none where the churches are more full and the sermons more empty than in America. There are magnificent exceptions, of course. But by and large, I am never hungrier and rarely angrier than when I come out of an American evangelical church after what passes for the preaching of the Word of God.

The problem is not just the heresy—though doubtless there is some of that. Nor is it just the degree of entertainment—and there is lots of that. Nor is it even the appalling gaps in the theology—for there is far too much of that. The real problem is that in what is said, there is almost no sense of announcement from God; and in what is shown, there is almost no sense of anointing by God.

Jeremiah attacked the false prophets of his day with the damning question, "Which of them has stood in the council of the LORD to see or to hear his word?" (Jeremiah 23:18). Are we who profess a high view of authority much better in practice? Is such a standard too demanding? I admit that my own expectations have been shaped decisively by the standards common when I came to Christ. As a student, I had the privilege of sitting under the ministry of D. Martyn Lloyd-Jones at his greatest. Before he preached every Sunday, he was alone for an hour with the Lord. Nobody disturbed him. If the Prime Minister arrived, someone else could greet him. If a person in crisis came, somebody else could counsel him. The pastor was with the King of kings. I do not remember Lloyd-Jones ever saying, "Thus saith the Lord." But he did not have to. His very bearing, quite apart from his words, showed that what he said was an announcement from God given with the anointing of God.

Loss of proclamation goes wider than preaching. Christian discourse in general is suffering. We have shifted from a proclamation style to a discussion style as part of our overall secularization, and the result is an endless proliferation of consultations, forums, seminars, symposiums, congresses and workshops. In most cases, old-fashioned proclamation would seem about as appropriate in those affairs as a full-throated obscenity, and no more likely.

The second requirement is *a visitation of the Spirit*. I use the old Puritan word *visitation* deliberately, because so many of the words describing revival have been devalued. We have no need of religious "resurgence," because that word is used of trends that are explicable in purely social terms. Nor can we be content to use the word "revival" merely as a synonym for "evangelism." And "visitation" is far beyond what is usually called "renewal." I am personally in favor of the renewal movement at its best, particularly where it touches personal worship, music forms, and so on. But even at its best, the renewal movement is a million miles short of true revival. Where is its note of profound conviction? Where is the wholesale changing of communities? Where is the developed passion for social holiness, as opposed to personal devotion?

Sadly, revival raises a question for many evangelicals: Do they believe in it still? Two years ago, Paul Weyrich, a leading conservative strategist, gave a speech called "Taking Stock." In it he argued, in effect, "Even if we conservatives win our entire agenda, we have lost." He shocked his audience further. "Yes," he said, "abortion, school prayer . . . Win them all, and we will still have failed." Why? Social change has changed too much, political change can change too little. Culture is flowing away faster than piecemeal action can remedy, short of a total cultural transformation of America.

Curiously, evangelicals a generation ago would have taken that as a truism, but in a day when political activism is in vogue, many who used to pray confidently, realistically, and practically for revival no longer have hunger for a visitation from God.

Show Me Your Glory

Let me draw the threads together. Do you know in your own life and in that of your local church: those two perspectives burnt into your mind, those two principles mastering your life, those two deficiencies highlighted so that you can avoid them, those two reminders spurring you on, and those two requirements before the world and the Lord? If so, I imagine you feel like many of us. Who is equal to the challenge? Can we really expect to see our culture turned around in our day?

Questions like these make me think of two men under pressure. One was the great German thinker, Max Weber. He never shut his eyes to the modern world. He wrestled with it, but the more he wrestled, the more pessimistic he became. One day a friend saw him pacing up and down, nearing the verge of a second breakdown.

"Max," he said, "why do you go on thinking like this when your conclusions leave you so depressed?"

Weber's reply has become a classic of intellectual commitment and courage, "I want to see how much I can stand."

Admirable in many respects, that is not the way for followers of Christ. We are not called to be tragic heroes or stoics or
spiritual masochists.

A very different response under pressure was that of
Moses. Faced by enemies behind, around, and ahead, and
finding discontent not only among his own people but within
his own family, he suddenly met the ultimate threat to his
people and to his task as leader: God himself. The Lord declared
that he would destroy the Israelites.

His very life and trust in God called into question, Moses
stood firm and countered the challenge by putting God on the
line (arguing the covenant), the people on the line (calling for
a consecration to the Lord even against families and friends),
and finally himself on the line (asking to be blotted out himself,
rather than the people).

Then, when the Lord had listened to his prayers, agreeing
first to forgive the people and then to come with them in person
rather than by an angel, Moses made his supreme request,
surely the most audacious prayer in all the Scriptures: "Show
me your glory." He wanted to know all of God that a fallen
sinner could be allowed to know, for nothing less would be
enough to see him through.

In that prayer, we have our answer to Nietzsche. When
God "dies" for a nation, a church, or an individual, a weightless-
ness results for which there is only one remedy—the glory of
God refilling them as the waters fill the sea. Wasn't that
Jeremiah's message to his generation? To a people who had
exchanged their glory for a god altogether nothing, he warned,
"Give glory to the LORD your God before he brings the dark-
ness" (Jeremiah 13:16).

G. K. Chesterton brought the same message to the United
States after his visit in 1921. The glory of the American republic,
he argued, had not been derived from itself and could not be
sustained by itself. Cut off from the source from which it
sprang, it would not long endure. He then concluded his book
with the magnificent line: "Freedom is the eagle whose glory
is gazing at the sun."

If we today stress the spiritual aspects of the gospel without the social, we lose all relevance in modern society. But if we stress the social without the spiritual, we lose our reality altogether. The ultimate factor in the church's engagement with society is the church's engagement with God.

Are we still tempted today to believe that we or anyone else can pull things around? We must forget it. On the other hand, are we overwhelmed by the task, overburdened by the state of the nation and the world? For God's sake, let us forget the eagle and ourselves and turn with Moses to the sun.

"Lord, show me your glory."

Chapter 4

The Christian and the Sanctity of Life

R. C. Sproul

*I*n every place I have been and have asked the question, How many of you want other people to treat you with dignity? the answer has been totally predictable. Every human being wants to be treated with dignity. And the reason we want to be *treated* with dignity is that we all have a profound conviction that we *have* dignity.

Knowing How and Knowing Why

Not long ago our organization held a series of meetings with a consultant who had been responsible for designing and bringing into being the Walt Disney Epcot Center in Orlando, Florida. He was exceedingly brilliant at focusing the efforts of an enterprise on the satisfactory completion of its announced objectives. In the course of our discussions this man said to our staff that there are only about 8 percent of the people in the work force who know how to do something that is significant and know how to do it well. "Those people never have to worry about a job," he said.

But he added, "That 8 percent, those who really know *how*, will always end up working for the person who knows *why*."

When Os Guinness urges us to root out the massive, anti-intellectual spirit that has paralyzed the power of Christianity in our day, he is striking at a real problem. We put very little stock in the importance of understanding why.

I have had countless people say to me, "Why do you give so much attention to this abstract question of the inerrancy of sacred Scripture? Why aren't you more activistically oriented?"

I usually reply, "It is because I despair of ever telling people in mass, 'You must rise up, stand in the gap, and prepare to die for the war against abortion [or some other Christian cause],' until I can say with authority that this is a summons that comes to us from God." We have lost our effectiveness in shaping the culture of this world because we have lost our authority. And that is why, I am convinced, we now march to suggestions and preferences, rather than to divine mandates.

What Is Man?

But my subject today is the sanctity of life, the dignity of humanity. And I want to ask: If you have dignity, as you no doubt think you do, *why* do you believe that you have it?

I have gone on record time and time again as being sharply critical of contemporary forms of philosophical humanism, not so much because I consider philosophical humanism irreligious, but because I consider it unintelligible. It is unintelligible to me that contemporary forms of humanism are able to manifest such extreme naivete from an intellectual viewpoint. Here is why I say that. The humanist is a person who goes about preaching, pleading, and crusading for human rights. A true humanist is a person who is profoundly concerned about the state and condition of human beings. True humanists care about the human situation. They elevate virtues such as honesty, integrity, compassion, and justice. They have been at the forefront of crusades for international human rights, civil rights, women's rights, and a host of other kinds of rights—while at the same time announcing to the world that they believe that human beings ultimately are entities that have emerged gratuitously from cosmic dust, as cosmic accidents, and who are destined inexorably to annihilation. They believe that human beings have come from the abyss of nothingness, live their poor hour on the stage, and then inevitably pass into the abyss of nonbeing.

That is the thought that drove Friedrich Nietzsche crazy. He believed that all we know and feel is only a manifestation of *das Nichtigkeit* ("nothingness"). This was also the motif of Martin Heidegger, who wrote that modern man's experience is rooted in what he called *geworfenheit*, that is, the sense of having been hurled chaotically into time and space with no intelligent beginning and no intelligent destiny.

Students of intellectual history know that the central metaphysical focus of the great minds of antiquity was the pursuit of ultimate reality, what they called the *ousia*, the "stuff" of reality. It preoccupied people like Parmenides, Heraclitus, Aristotle, and Plato. It caused Socrates to say that the "unexamined life" is not worth living.

But then, as variant systems of metaphysics came into collision with each other, the attention of philosophers became fixed on issues of epistemology. They said, "Before we can discover what truth is, we have to ask: How is truth to be discerned?" Is it through minds speculating rationally, deductively and logically, or is it through observation, empirical testing and experimentation? At this point the "how" of knowing came to the center of the stage.

That quest ended in a certain kind of skepticism. But in the nineteenth century, philosophers came up with a new focus: the meaning of history. Is history the concrete unfolding in space and time of the absolute spirit in a dialectical process of theses clashing with antitheses and being raised up into new syntheses, as Hegel suggested? Or is it the concrete dollars-and-cents battles of the economics of dialectical materialism, as Marx suggested?

It is no accident that the central absorbing question of contemporary   intellectual   investigation   is   no   longer metaphysics or epistemology or even the philosophy of history. The abiding question of our day is anthropology, because the humanist, in his naivete, has been crusading for human rights with his feet firmly planted, as Francis Schaeffer was fond of saying, in thin air. He is on an intellectual roller coaster without brakes, because he says that man has come from nothing and goes to nothing. Those are the two poles of his existence. His origin is insignificant. His destiny is insignificant. And yet, so they say, "In between man is wonderful."

If you are a humanist and think about that—I would say for ten seconds—you will be driven to absolute despair. It is because you will have to listen to the hard questions of the atheistic existentialist who looks you straight in the face and says, "Don't give me this superficial sentimental nonsense about human rights. Why should I care about whether black germs or white germs sit in the back of the bus? If I come from nothing and I go to nothing, I might as well sleep in tomorrow. Why should I care about what's happening in the Gulag thousands of miles away from here or in the abortion clinics down the street. Who cares about undifferentiated masses of protoplasm, if we are nothing but cosmic accidents?"

That is the great issue in the school system today—not what year the universe came into being or whether it was six days or six million days that God took to create the world. The issue that is dominating discussion in the public schools today is: Is man a cosmic accident? If life is an idiot's tale, full of sound and fury, signifying nothing, can we ever have dignity?

Intrinsic or Extrinsic Dignity?

But let me say this. If somebody should come to me and say, "R. C., do you believe that you have intrinsic dignity?" I would answer, "Of course . . . *not*! Such an idea is unthinkable for a Christian. On the contrary, there is nobody in this world who has *intrinsic* dignity." Did you catch that all important adjective? I did not just say, "People do not have dignity." I believe people do have dignity. But—this is my point—they do not have intrinsic dignity.

What is intrinsic dignity? Intrinsic dignity is that which is eternally built into the very nature of the entity itself. We do not have that, and I am going to tell you why. And, at the same time, I am going to try to explain why I believe that people do have dignity. I am going to answer by reference to Genesis 1:25-27.

> God made the wild animals according to their kinds, the livestock according to their kinds, and all the creatures that move along the ground according to their kinds. And God saw that it was good.
>
> Then God said, "Let us make man in our image, in our likeness, and let them rule over the fish of the sea and the birds of the air, over the livestock, over all the earth, and over all the creatures that move along the ground."
>
> So God created man in his own image, in the image of God he created him; male and female he created them.

Then verse 7 of Genesis 2:

> The LORD God formed the man from the dust of the ground and breathed into his nostrils the breath of life, and the man became a living being.

Os Guinness has explained the Hebrew meaning of the word *glory*, showing that, when God created the universe, he assigned a glory to the stars, and a glory to the moon, and a glory to the sun, and a glory to the man, and a glory to the woman. If we look carefully at the meaning of that word *glory* (*kabod* in the Old Testament, *doxa* in the New Testament) we see that its root meaning is "heaviness." This is the foundational concept from which the Latin term, *dignitas*, from which we get our word *dignity*, is derived. When we talk about human dignity, we are saying that human beings have dignity, value, or significance because there is something weighty about them.

Sometimes we hear the other side of it, of course—that "all men are like grass" (Isaiah 40:6). We wither and die. Human life is like the chaff which even small zephyrs—minute currents of wind—can carry away, because it lacks weight. The Bible is acutely conscious of the fragile character of life, on the one hand. We are mortal, vulnerable, susceptible to death. Therein is our "lightness."

But God also says that there is a weightiness to being human, because he assigns value, significance, or weight to human life. You and I do not have *intrinsic* dignity. There is only One who possesses that eternal weight of glory in himself, One alone who is intrinsically kabod. Nevertheless, on the very first page of our Bibles, this uniquely glorious God says, "I'll make a man in my own image. I'll stoop down to the dirt, form it, and breathe a bit of my life into it." So God did. That worthless bit of dust, which had no intrinsic dignity belonging to itself whatsoever, became—the Scriptures tell us—"a living being." That lifeless bit of mud began to move, throb, think, choose, act, care, and love—all because God stamped it with himself.

Our dignity is *extrinsic*. It is derived, dependent, contingent. Yet it is very, very real.

No Creation, No Dignity

Here is the bottom line: No creation, no dignity. I learned a long time ago that it is impossible to have your cake and eat it too, which is what the modern humanist wants to do—but can only do as long as we fail to require him to think.

Now note what Genesis 9:1-6 tells us about human dignity:

> Then God blessed Noah and his sons, saying to them, "Be fruitful and increase in number and fill the earth. The fear and dread of you will fall upon all the beasts of the earth and all the birds of the air, upon every creature that moves along the ground,

and upon all the fish of the sea; they are given into your hands. Everything that lives and moves will be food for you. Just as I gave you the green plants, I now give you everything.

"But you must not eat meat that has its lifeblood still in it. And for your lifeblood I will surely demand an accounting. I will demand an accounting from every animal. And from each man, too, I will demand an accounting for the life of his fellow man.

"Whoever sheds the blood of man,
    by man shall his blood be shed;
    for in the image of God
    has God made man."

In the Hebrew text the words "Whoever sheds the blood of man, by man shall his blood be shed" are not a future prediction. They are a categorical imperative. They indicate that in the covenant that God made with Noah following the Flood, God established a law requiring the execution of those who are guilty of murder in the first degree.

Those who want to say that God never ordained capital punishment are committed to a course of sheer despair in exegesis. A person would have to refuse to hear the Word of God quite deliberately and willfully to miss something as clearly stated in Scripture as that. We cannot deny that, at least at this one point in human history, God Almighty ordained, instituted, commanded the death penalty for those who commit first degree murder.

But here again is my question—because this discussion is not chiefly about capital punishment or about any of the other closely related problems that are hanging in the balance in our society today. I only ask you to focus on this: *Why* did God institute capital punishment, at least in the days of Noah? *Why* did God say that the murderer must be put to death? The answer is given in the verses I just quoted: "in the image of God has God made man."

I remember when the state of Pennsylvania's legislature reintroduced capital punishment, and it was vetoed by Governor Milton Shapp. The governor gave this explanation for his veto: "I vetoed capital punishment because God says, 'Thou shalt not kill.'" I am grateful the governor of Pennsylvania wanted to exercise his office under the authority of God and wanted to obey God by abolishing capital punishment in Pennsylvania. And I am delighted that he had at least read Exodus 20:13 in his Bible. But I am sorry he didn't read Exodus 21 or 22. In fact, I wonder if he even read Exodus 20. Because everybody knows what the Old Testament prescription was for those who violated the commandment, "Thou shalt not kill." They were to be killed.

Why? Was it because the Jewish people had a low view of human life?

No! The rationale for God's ordaining capital punishment in the days of Noah was because of the *sanctity* of life. God said, "The blood of the man who has shed blood shall be shed, because the one he murdered was made in my image."

Do you see what is going on here? The reason why human life is so valuable—why there is so much dignity assigned to every human being—is that, when God prints his image on a human creature, that image is so precious, so sacred, that if somebody willfully and malevolently kills that person, God considers it an assault upon himself. It is an attack on *his* life—because every human being bears the image of God. I may not like every human being. I may not agree with every human being. But I have an absolute obligation to work for, protect and, if necessary, die for the preservation of the dignity of each one.

The theme of Congress on the Bible II and the subtitle of this book is "a call to action." So let me conclude by saying this: *Any country that is willing to kill its unborn children for a fee is a godless nation.*

I am supposed to be a theologian by profession, maybe with not all the dignity a theologian is supposed to manifest—

and maybe no one will take me seriously—but I have had the privilege of being able to study the things of God as my life's vocation. I am sure there are errors in my theology. If I knew where they were, I would try to get rid of them. I know I am not accurate or faithful all the time, though I want to be. But I do know this. If I know anything about the character of Almighty God, whose person and work I have been studying for so many years, I know that God hates abortion on demand.

Do you know that?

Apparently, not all evangelicals—not to mention all Christians—do. Abortion is commonplace in our culture. But what gives me a heavy heart—the reason I go to bed at night with a heavy heart—is because this is happening, not only in the secular world that does not know God, but in the evangelical church. There are evangelical preachers and teachers saying, "Abortion is all right, because a woman has a right to her own body." No she doesn't! I say to anyone who says that a woman has a right to do with her own body what she wants to do with it, "Tell me where she got that right. Where did it come from?" The only place rights can come from is from God. So if we find ourselves saying, "I have the right to do this," claiming divine endorsement for something when God has expressly forbidden it, we are calling good "evil" and evil "good." We are saying that God endorses an activity that he actually abominates, and we are in deep trouble.

I cannot believe that all Christians are not literally screaming, "Bloody murder!" every day. Because when we allow this to happen, we have surrendered the sanctity of human life.

Chapter 5

The Christian and God's World

James I. Packer

I am not an American. I am British by birth and Canadian by choice. But though I am not an American, I feel it to be an enormous privilege, as well as a tremendous responsibility, to be addressing Americans on the theme of the guidance that a trusted Bible gives for action—corrective, visionary, reforming, prophetic, evangelical, salt-and-light action in community life today.

The Battle for America's Soul

Why do I feel this so strongly? Why, because of the uniquely significant vocation that God appears to have given to the United States of America in the modern world.

Theologians, as you know, distinguish between *special* grace, the grace that saves sinners by turning them to Christ and that builds up the church in and through Christ, and *common* grace, the grace of providential action—sometimes kindly, sometimes severe—that restrains sin, maintains some order and some justice in our fallen communities, and so provides a milieu in which the gospel and the work of special grace can go forward. When Paul directs Christians to pray for rulers "that we [believers] may live peaceful and quiet lives in all godliness and holiness" (1 Timothy 2:2), his words clearly express this view of common grace serving the interests of special grace.

I see the United States as having at this time a unique role in the world at both levels of divine operation. I might perhaps be able to see this more clearly than a native American ever could, simply because I look at it from outside. As a non-American, I do not endorse any form of that utopian triumphalism, the secular counterpart of the Pilgrims' hope of building new Jerusalem in Massachusetts, that periodically breaks surface in the American mind and that looks to outsiders so ominously like the pride that goes before a fall. The idea that America is God's most favored nation and always will be is a snare and a delusion that can only sap America's spiritual strength in the way that Aleksandr Solzhenitsyn and Malcolm Muggeridge think has happened already. Do not, I beg you, fall victim to any such notion as that.

Nonetheless, I want to go on record as saying to you, and about you, the two things that now follow, and I ask you to hear me well.

First, as regards *special grace*. The United States of America is a nation of almost a quarter of a billion people. Of these, 65 percent claim a church connection, and something between twenty and forty million—maybe one in ten, maybe one in five—profess to be born again evangelical Christians. The United States has a conversionist folk religion that gives great support to evangelism. (I say that with feeling, as I think any Western European would, for in our native countries the folk religion is formal and formalistic, and greatly obstructs evangelism.)

During the forty-three years of my Christian life, the work of evangelism in America, both in local churches and in larger crusades, has been advancing apace, and the fruit of this advance now shows in many striking ways. Evangelical churches and seminaries, many of them founded within the past generation, are crowded out. Evangelical literature has never sold so well. At no time for more than a century has the evangelical profile been higher. Impressive young people keep emerging, on the way to leadership in tomorrow's church. Also, a great deal of money constantly becomes available to finance evangelical churches, plus a vast array of evangelical parachurch ministries and overseas missions too.

Of no other human unit of comparable size anywhere in the world can these things be said. In Britain and Australia, it is estimated that 1 to 2 percent of the population are evangelical Christians—certainly not more—and the supply of manpower for missionary work has dwindled to a trickle. In continental Europe, things are on the whole worse. In Africa and Latin America, the number of professed Christians grows by the million, but inner instabilities, political agonies, and grinding economic hardships make it impossible for the Christian communities to become a major missionary force beyond their own doorsteps. The evangelical church in China—whether computed at ten or fifty million, or somewhere between those two extreme estimates—lives under permanent political threat and, in any case, is too poor and too geographically static to be able to spread the gospel in any significant way outside its own country. The same seems to be true of the big evangelical constituency in Korea and the smaller one in India.

What it boils down to is that among the larger nations, only the United States has both the manpower and the money to sustain evangelical world mission for the next generation, and this gives America a uniquely important role in the global strategy of the kingdom of God at the present time.

Then, second, as regards *common grace*. The United States of America has in the providence of God effectively become, since World War II, both the police force and the defense force of the entire non-Communist world. Whether this role is always fulfilled in the best way is something about which we can argue. But there can be no argument about the fact that the role now exists, and that the American people have accepted it. The isolationist noises that floated across the Atlantic when I was a boy are no longer heard, for today's Americans see themselves as having an obligation—many would soberly say, a God-given obligation—to try, at least, to be the world's peacekeeper and a bulwark against Marxist advance. In light of the typical hostility of Marxist regimes to the Christian gospel, the importance of America's role for preserving religious liberty and an open arena for world wide evangelism is too obvious to need discussion.

From these facts, I conclude that America has a central and crucial place, at two levels—not just one—in the contemporary Christian world mission.

How important it is then that America's inner spiritual resources be strong enough to sustain this dual role. And how certain it is that Satan will seek by every means in his power to undermine America's spiritual resources, so that the nation falls down on the job. And how inescapable, to me at least, is the conclusion that the capture over the past half-century by the imperialist ideology called "secular humanism" of America's media establishment, its educational establishment, its literary and artistic establishments, its medical, socio-economic and legal establishments—in short just about all its character-shaping and opinion-making structures apart from the evangelical church itself—has been one of Satan's strategic maneuvers, a well-conceived and sadly successful one, against the kingdom of God.

A few days ago, a European colleague of mine at Regent College said to me, in words that I find prophetic, "The battle for the soul of America is just about to begin." I took his thought to be that all the separating out of Christian and post-Christian standpoints during the last several decades (which in this regard have felt tense enough, God knows, to many of us) has been merely preliminary to the really decisive encounter—a clash that remains future but cannot now be far off. Hitherto, the forces of secularism and humanism, on the one hand, and of biblical Christianity, on the other, have been positioning themselves—more truly perhaps than either side has yet realized—for direct confrontation. The clash will be between the uninhibited materialistic egoism of the full-blown secularist, in which the only values recognized are one's own pleasure, profit, and power ("the lust of the flesh, and the lust of the eyes, and the pride of life," as the King James Version of 1 John 2:16 called them) and the consistent theocentric altruism of the thoroughgoing Christian, in which the supreme value of my neighbor to God, and therefore to me, determines all personal relations and all social policy.

Outsiders see American society as prone to push ideas to extremes, and there is no question that materialistic pragmatism, based on relativistic morals, is being pushed to extremes in the United States today. Henceforth, it would seem, sustained ideological conflict must be expected, assuming—as I do assume— that biblical Christians in the United States will not raise their hands in meek surrender before the secular humanist juggernaut.

When I posit as one of the contending viewpoints a consistent theocentric altruism—that is, a God-honoring concern for the welfare of all other human beings before oneself—I am not, I confess, looking in the direction of neoliberal Protestantism or neomodernist Catholicism, free though both those movements have been with that sort of language. Both lose touch, more or less, with the biblical view of my neighbor's nature and need. Both as a result become half-way houses to humanism of the secular sort. And on moral questions in society, both tend to end up kicking the ball through their own goal. (Think of neoliberalism's support of violence in the name of peace and of its expressed views on, for instance, divorce and remarriage, abortion, and homosexuality.)

No, what I have in mind is a realistic commitment of conscience to the actual spiritual values and moral absolutes of Scripture and Scripture's Christ—a commitment, therefore, to care for my neighbor without limit because he bears God's image, even though I do not believe in his natural goodness, as perhaps he himself does, and even though he may be weak or handicapped or sexually misaligned or guilty of major crime or as yet unborn. To be frank, it is only among those who trust their Bible absolutely that I expect ever to see commitment of this quality.

When my colleague anticipated escalating confrontations between biblical Christianity and empire-building secularism, I think he read the signs of the times correctly. They are, to my mind, ominous. I have to agree with those who see secularism as so deeply entrenched already in the places of power that loosening its grip must require at least a generation of all-out argument, no matter how right-minded and God-blessed that arguing may be. I have to agree also with those who doubt whether evangelicals generally have perceived the gravity of the issues that are currently at stake, or the extent of the pressure (mostly indirect as yet) that society is in the process of mounting against nonrelativist biblical belief. Chesterton's words express what I am forced to say as I look at the big picture of North America:

> I bring you naught for your comfort,
> Yea, naught for your desire,
> Save that the sky grows darker yet,
> And the wind rises higher.

From all that I have said, you can see why, at just this moment in the battle for the soul of the most influential nation on earth, I count it a huge privilege, as well as a huge responsibility, to be speaking to you about these things.

My subject is "The Christian and God's World." But although this has been a long introduction, this is, in fact, what I have been discussing from the start. So far I have offered only contemporary analysis and comment, however. What I aim to do now is to set my mapping of this field of Christian responsibility on a directly biblical basis. In what follows, I shall be discussing in order each of these four alliterated realities: the *concept* of God's world, the *creation* of God's world, the *corruption* of God's world, and the Christian's *calling* in God's world. By this means, I seek to deepen our insight into the present-day tensions upon which I have been dwelling thus far.

The Concept of God's World

I speak first, then, of the concept of God's world, that is, of the world *as God's*. My point here is simply that in the sense in which it is God's, it is not ours, and we must not slip into the bad habit of supposing that we own it and may therefore deal with it any way we like.

When we say "world," it is clear that we are referring in a general way to all that surrounds us—spatially, temporally, and relationally. But what do we mean when we add the possessive adjective and speak of "*our* world"? If we are thinking in physical and geographical terms, "our world" will signify this planet, with its chemical structure, climatic laws, limited resources, vast population and so on. If we are thinking in racial and anthropological terms, "our world" will signify people of all nations. If we are thinking historically and culturally, "our world" will signify the state of things in this particular era. If our focus is personal and subjective, "our world" will signify things as they appear to each of us from the vantage point (or through the blinders) of each one's private knowledge, beliefs, and interests, so that each of us truly lives, as we say, in a "world" of our own. But whichever of these specific meanings is in view, the use of "our" is man-centered and, therefore, from one standpoint at least, dangerously improper. Why? Because it is not really our world in any sense at all. God made it, God sustains it, God owns it, God keeps it, God rules it, and we are part of it.

Between them, the biblical words for "world" cover approximately the same range of meanings that our English word does, but always with a theological, God-centered perspective. The biblical vision is of the world as belonging to God and of ourselves as, at most, his stewards, bailiffs, agents, lieutenants

and trustees—his regents, as we say at Regent College—
charged to manage God's world for him according to his revealed will.

God putting Adam to tend a garden perfectly pictures our
God-given cultural task. We are to see the entire created order,
including, of course, our neighbors and ourselves, as the estate
that we, as God's gardeners, are responsible for cultivating.
Sometimes this responsibility is called the "cultural mandate,"
meaning mankind's obligation to develop a pattern of corporate
life that honors the Creator by embodying true moral and
spiritual values and so furthers the realizing of all the joyful
potential of human life in God's world.

Never forget that the glory of God and the happiness of
man were always meant to go together! Where you truly have
the former, you will truly have the latter also. A necessary
element in any realistic plan to reducing the sum of present
human misery is a return to the cultural mandate.

The humanism that we face treats the world and everything and everyone in the world irreligiously, and sees this as
a mark of maturity, as if by deleting the divine you come of
age. We must be clear that this attitude expresses not maturity
but apostasy and needs to be challenged at every point. After
all, were God not upholding the world in being, no humanist
would exist to deny him. It cannot be said too often that this
world is in every sense God's world, which his human creatures
must learn to handle reverently, for his praise.

The Creation of God's World

Now to my second topic, the creation of God's world.
Here my purpose is to plead for a worthy testimony to the
wonders of the Creator's work.

Come with me, then, to the first chapter of the Bible,
and observe that there we are shown God bringing into being
a world-*order*. The achieving of order out of dark and formless
chaos is the central story line of Genesis 1:1—2:3. It is natural
to conclude that the "goodness" that God tells us he saw in

each thing he formed and in the finished work of creation as a whole (Genesis 1:4, 10, 12, 18, 21, 25, 31) lay partly, at least, in the fact that every item represented a step forward in the excluding of chaos and the establishing of order. A further natural conclusion is that God gave us Genesis 1 as the highly formalized narrative it is partly, at least, to underline for us the fact that he loves order and sees beauty in it, and is in every sense a God of order, as opposed to randomness and confusion.

Beyond this very basic point, Genesis 1 is tricky ground for interpreters to walk on, as we all know. But I will venture a little further. The following perspectival observations should surely command general assent.

First, *the chapter celebrates the fact of creation and the power, wisdom, and goodness of the Creator, on whom attention centers throughout.* Though many of God's creatures are mentioned by name as the narrative unfolds, what is being said at each stage is not "meet the *creation* " (as if we had never met it before), but rather "meet the *Creator!*" From our knowledge of the marvelous complexity of all the creatures that are listed we are to gauge their Maker's glory and adore him accordingly.

Second, *the style of the chapter is imaginative, pictorial, poetic, and doxological* (glory-giving, in the manner of worship), rather than clinically and prosaically descriptive in the deadpan scientific fashion. It is, after all, as we said, ceremonial celebration, telling us who made the world and each item within it, rather than how in detail he produced each effect.

Third, *the Earth-centeredness of the presentation reflects* not scientific naivete about the solar system, but *theological interest in man's uniqueness and responsibility under God on this planet.*

Fourth, *the pastoral and edificatory purpose of the narrative is to show its readers their own place and calling in God's world* and the abiding significance of the sabbath as a memorial of creation—not to satisfy academic or technical curiosity about the distant past.

No interpretation of Genesis 1 that ignores these built-in perspectives can be right, nor can it be other than a majoring in minors, for these are the angles that are important. Within them, to be sure, it is legitimate to ask how the six days of creation relate to shifting scientific theories of origins. Various hypotheses are offered. None of these, however, is more than an educated guess. So none should expect ever to have the field to itself, and each should be put forward with modesty and tolerance toward other views.

It is another victory for Satan when Bible-believers go for each other's throats over their rival notions of what the sciences say about the six days of creation and what the text says about the ideas of the scientists. Such infighting is a luxury that, pressed as we are by the secularist squeeze of which I spoke earlier, we can neither justify nor afford. Tenacity of belief that all the Bible is true does not require equal tenacity in believing that all one's own ideas about its meaning in disputed areas are true also. And in the case of Genesis 1, a worthy echo of its witness to the Creator's glory becomes impossible if all we let ourselves think about when interpreting it is Bible-and-science questions. A worthy witness to the reality of the Creator, one that links up compellingly with the sense of creatureliness that is indelibly inscribed on every human heart, is what we most need today.

The Corruption of God's World

My third theme, the corruption of God's world, requires me to narrow my focus from the world in the sense of the entire cosmos to the world in the sense of our race in rebellion, organized without God and indeed against God, and hence unfriendly to basic biblical values. "The world" in this sense of hell-bent humanity is, of course, a frequent focus of the New Testament, where Christian conflict with the world is a recurring theme. My purpose here is to do just one thing, namely, to spotlight the motivation that drives the world in its self- affirming, anti-God courses of action. For that, I take you to the story of the tower of Babel in Genesis 11:1-9, where the totalitarian dynamics of the fallen human collective are pictured with supreme starkness.

What drives the world? Pride, plus pride's daughter, paranoia—the sense of being constantly threatened unless one can collar more power than one has at the moment. Augustine analyzed "original sin" as pride (*superbia*), the passion to be "top person," independent, self-sufficient, big, strong and, thus, secure. And surely he was right. No profounder analysis is possible, for this is the very heart—the heart of the heart, we might say—of the "play-God, fight-God, kill-God" syndrome that infected our race in Eden and rules the unregenerate still.

The project planned on the plain of Shinar illustrates this perfectly: "Come, let us build ourselves a city, with a tower that reaches to the heavens, so that we may make a name for ourselves and not be scattered over the face of the whole earth" (v. 4). There was bravado here. The project was grandiose to the point of goofiness. They were going to build a great city and a skyscraper tower within it as a symbol of its strength, and all they had to work with was crude makeshift materials—homemade bricks instead of quarried stone, and bitumen (surface tar) instead of proper mortar. But the prospect of power intoxicated them, so that they lost the capacity to calculate what was realistically possible and what was not. (One thinks of Hitler's boast that his Third Reich would last a thousand years. It actually staggered along for twelve before defeat in World War II put an end to it.) Buoyed up by the feeling that if everyone pulled together there was no limit to what they could do, these starry-eyed devotees of earthly glory set themselves to establish the greatest power base ever.

The pride that spawns all centralized collectivism and all totalitarian empire building was never more clearly expressed. Scattered, we stumble and suffer, they reasoned. But by our solidarity, we stand and are safe! The world still thinks in these terms.

In due course, we read, "The LORD came down to see the city and the tower that the men were building" (v. 5). He gave the project a run for its money, so that its perversity might clearly appear before he finally frustrated it by confusing the builders' language, making it impossible for them to cooperate any more and so bringing about the very scattering that they had hoped to avoid (cp. vv. 4 and 8).

Such is still his way. To preserve an environment in which gospel godliness is at least possible, he regularly breaks up ungodly unions, brings down power blocs, and causes the same pride that first drew sinners together in empire building to push them apart in misunderstanding and mistrust of each other. This pattern of divine action, which from one point of view is merited judgment—dealing with sin as it deserves—is from another point of view common grace, restraining sin from doing as much damage as it otherwise would. God will not let his world be spoiled or his Word suppressed beyond a certain point, and his partial, if not total, restraint of sin in the structures of society will continue to operate till Antichrist comes.

Meantime, it remains a natural urge in fallen humanity to band together to create units of power and to require unqualified commitment and total loyalty to those units. That is both the proof and the measure of the world's corruption. Those who direct the world's political, economic, and ideological power plays may be expected constantly to feel that the biblical Christian's loyalty to Scripture and its God is a threat to them. Paranoia will then take over, and what the Puritan, Richard Baxter, in the title of one of his books, called *Cain and Abel Malignity*, will express itself against faithful believers over and over again. We must be prepared for this.

The Christian's Calling in the World

My fourth theme is the Christian's calling in the world. How should the Bible-believers of the secularized West respond to the pressures under which the world puts them? How should they position themselves in relation to politics, economics, poverty, the arts, conservation, education and the many other spheres of human concern in which sub- and anti-Christian attitudes have become dominant?

Let me clear the ground by dismissing at once three inadequate responses to such pressures, all of which were embodied in persons whom we meet in the gospel story and none of which was endorsed by Jesus himself. Palestine was enemy-occupied territory, just as this world is, the Romans being the enemy in the one case and Satan in the other, and different Jews responded to the dominance of the Romans in different ways.

The Zealots embraced the way of *confrontation*: they sought the overthrow of Rome in holy war and the replacing of Rome's rule by a kingdom of saints, in which only loyal Jews would find a place. They showed no interest in the non-political kingdom of God that Jesus preached.

The Sadducees took the way of *compromise*: they reasoned that since they could not beat the Romans, they had better join them. So they greedily grasped and hung on to such crumbs of power as the Romans threw them and cynically settled for liquidating Jesus, lest he so disturb things that their little bit of power would be forfeit.

Finally, the Pharisees followed the path of *separation*: they withdrew from all associations that they thought defiled them and would not touch any sphere of life in which the Romans were publicly in control.

Thus, the Zealots never made common cause with the world, the Sadducees never challenged the world, and the Pharisees never got involved with the world. All three attitudes have their counterpart today, as you know.

But Jesus and the apostles saw none of these paths as proper for Christians in this fallen world. Rather, they set before us in essence the original cultural mandate, pointed up by the four imperatives that follow:

Discern what is good and what is bad about the world . As we saw earlier, God made the cosmic order genuinely good. When Paul says, "Everything God created is good" (1 Timothy 4:4), he is merely echoing Genesis 1. It is the Manichaean heresy to affirm that the world of matter, physical life, and sensory pleasure is valueless and evil. Down the centuries that heresy has haunted Christian minds and produced many ugly things: a false antithesis between the material and the spiritual; false guilt about enjoying food, physical comfort, and sex in marriage; glorification of dirt, seediness, and uncouthness; pride in one's world-denying asceticism; contracting out of the arts and all cultural endeavor ("not spiritual, you know"); and so on. But the truth of the goodness of creation teaches us to negate all such nastiness (for such it really is), and that we must learn to do.

However, the other side of the truth here is that the world of mankind has become genuinely bad through the moral and spiritual twisting of human nature. "The play is the tragedy Man," and the tragedy centers in the fact that our sinfulness is precisely good gone wrong, nobility befouled, real value really wasted. The bitter fruit of the fall is that now human relations are disrupted (Cain kills Abel, and Lamech proclaims jungle law as early as Genesis 4); people exploit and swindle each other and enjoy inflicting cruelty and violence; community structures are disrupted by self-seeking; science is made to serve selfish ambition; the fine arts are used to undermine morality; and the nightmarish state of things summarized in Romans 1:26-31 is found to be a realistic description of all societies at all times.

The created values of human life must not be confused with its acquired corruptions, nor must the requirements of righteousness be forgotten as we focus on the habits of fallen mankind—or we shall never know how to act rightly in God's world. Unprincipled acquiescence in corrupt manners and customs, based on the assumption that whatever is, is right, is not the way to go, and we must not allow thoughtless empathy to make us imagine that it is.

Understand Christian liberty and responsibility in the world. The freedom of the Christian was a New Testament and Reformation emphasis that is often obscured today. What it meant was that Christians are not bound to the law in any form as a system of salvation, nor to any of the typical rites and restrictions that God imposed under the old covenant (cf. Galatians 4:21—5:1, 13), and that no use of created things for enrichment and enjoyment is defiling, provided the user shows gratitude to the God from whom these benefits come (1 Timothy 4:3-5).

But this privilege of drawing joy from what one now knows to be one's Father's world must be exercised responsibly; otherwise, we sin. Responsible use of freedom limits one's action to what is helpful spiritually to oneself and others (1 Corinthians 6:12; 8:9, 13; 10:23, 31-11:1). It restricts one to what best serves the glory of God and the good of others, and forbids one to let the merely permissible become the enemy of that best, elbowing it out for the sake of a lesser good. It will often be a more responsible use of freedom to say no to the permissible, just because it would not have a good effect on others, than to say yes to it just in order to make the point that it is indeed permitted under the gospel. Christian liberty must never be swallowed up by subcultural legalism, but neither may it ever degenerate into sub-Christian license. We shall never know how to act rightly in God's world until we are clear on this.

Distinguish the use from the misuse of the world. "Using" the world (Paul's phrase, 1 Corinthians 7:31) means dealing constructively with the people and the resources that constitute one's personal environment. It means involvement, planning, and toil in the task of creating wisdom, welfare, and wealth for oneself and others. Misusing or abusing the world means being enslaved by these activities so that, in effect, they become our idols and we live for them as activities, rather than seeing them as means of honoring and praising the God who led us to them.

Enslavement to activities is worldliness in its purest form: the compulsive workaholism that I described is as worldly as is any form of laziness. It needs to be better understood than it sometimes is that whether persons are worldly or not depends not on how much pleasure they take from life, but on the spirit in which they take it. If we let pleasant things engross us so that we forget God, we are worldly. If we receive them gratefully with a purpose of pleasing God by our appreciation and use of his gifts, we are not worldly but godly. Worldliness is the spirit that substitutes earthly goals (pleasure, profit, popularity, privilege, power) for life's true goal, which is the praise of God. For a human being to receive praise is not worldly, but it is worldly to angle for praise and applause, to find one's highest happiness in having people compliment and admire you and to lose sight of the fact that the ultimate recipient of praise for all the good things humans are praised for should always be the Creator himself. Only when the peril of worldliness is truly understood and avoided, and the nonworldly use of the world is truly practiced, can our commerce with the created order become a fulfillment of the Creator's calling to Christian believers.

Value the people as distinct from the ways of the world. Society's ways are bad, due to sin, and people need to be rescued from them. Jude was making this point very bluntly when he said: "Snatch others from the fire and save them; to others show mercy, mixed with fear—hating even the clothing stained by corrupted flesh" (Jude 23). Redirecting the misdirected lives of those whom our grandfathers called "precious souls" belongs to the work of evangelism, which is always the first and basic form of social service and the first item of the Christian calling in the secular community. Loving sinners and hating their sins, sharing our faith with them to save them from the fire while feeling awed horror at the despite done to God by the filthy things they have dabbled in, is the prime task that God sets his people in every age, and no amount of concern for wider cultural involvements must be allowed to displace it from its priority.

Cultural endeavor without evangelism is one stage worse than evangelism without cultural endeavor, for the concentration on evangelism does at least put first things first. But evangelism with cultural endeavor, making common cause with others when they fight for what is right in society, while mounting opposition against them when they go after what is wrong, is the proper formula for fulfilling the Christian's calling in God's world.

I do not say that the discharge of this dual mandate can be made easy or straightforward. I know that in our day at least, it cannot. The Western societies in which we are called to serve God as his stewards of creation and his Samaritans to those in spiritual and material need are whirling maelstroms of sectional selfishness, economic exploitation, utopian unrealism, crushing collectivism, rival power plays, moral cynicism and manipulative corner cutting at every turn. Such conditions are bound constantly to hamper and thwart us, but they must never induce us to stop. It is our business to persist faithfully in our God-given role in the world as the salt that preserves it and the light that guides it, and not to be daunted if our labor feels like a drop in a bucket that makes no difference at all. One day our Master's "Well done" will more than make amends for any discouragements that we may suffer here and now.

And should not that be enough for us?

Let us, like Nehemiah, first pray, and then give ourselves to our task.

Chapter 6

The Christian and Biblical Justice

John M. Perkins

*M*y subject is "The Christian and Biblical Justice." But I need to begin by telling you what happened in 1957 when a sixty-year-old white lady started a Child Evangelism Fellowship Bible Club in the black community of Monrovia, California. A four-year-old boy went to that Bible club and heard the gospel of Jesus Christ for the first time. His life was changed, and they soon got him into a black Sunday school in the neighborhood. Each week he would go home excitedly and tell his father about it. Out of curiosity, the father went to see this Sunday school, and for the first time he also heard the gospel and was converted. I was that father.

I had gone to Monrovia after my brother had been killed in a racial incident in Mississippi, where I was born. I had spent the first seventeen years of my life in Mississippi, and when I left, I was hoping never to return. My mother had died when I was just seven months old, and my father had given his five children to his mother, who had already raised nineteen children of her own.

We lived on the old plantation system, which was developed to hold black people in segregation after Emancipation.

We were sharecroppers until the system was broken in 1964, as an outgrowth of the equal rights movement. I dropped out of school somewhere between the third and fifth grades, and never went back to school because I was needed to work on the plantation.

After my conversion to Jesus Christ in California, I felt called of God to return to the place of my birth. I knew there were many people like me who had been through many religious exercises but who had never understood the simple gospel message—that Jesus Christ could live out his life in a person.

In this way my pilgrimage to be a Christian and to live out biblical justice began.

Definition of a Christian

What is a Christian? A Christian is a person who has repented of his or her sin and has asked God's forgiveness; one who has decided to be a follower of Jesus Christ, a disciple, a learner; one who desires to do the will of God and to pattern his or her life on Christ's. In Galatians 2:20 the apostle Paul describes his understanding of what it means to be a Christian in these words: "I have been crucified with Christ and I no longer live, but Christ lives in me. The life I live in the body, I live by faith in the Son of God, who loved me and gave himself for me."

Paul is saying that Christ's death for sin was his death, Christ's resurrection was his new life, and the life he was living was because of a new power: Christ's life within him. He credits this new life to his belief in the Son of God, who gave himself for him.

Galatians 2:20 leaves little doubt that Paul had experienced new life and that this change had come about as a result of Paul's having believed in Jesus Christ. We can conclude, then, that one becomes a Christian by faith. This is also what the Bible teaches elsewhere. The Bible says that "without faith it is impossible to please God" and that "anyone who comes to him must believe that he exists and that he rewards those who earnestly seek him" (Hebrews 11:6). We are taught that "the righteous will live by faith" (Romans 1:17). This faith is born in obedience to the Word of God. It is when one hears the Word of God, believes it, acts upon it, trusts in it, and orders his or her life according to it that one is saved. One is saved by faith alone. But the evidence of saving faith is obedience to the Word of God.

Abraham is the father of our faith. He earned this title because he heard the voice of God and moved out in obedience to the Word of God. Abraham's obedience was the evidence of his salvation. The Bible says that "faith by itself, if it is not accompanied by action, is dead" (James 2:17). Therefore, a Christian is one who has responded actively to the Word of God.

Another element in the conversion experience of the apostle Paul is that his salvation was an initiative taken by God through Christ—in the sense that Jesus loved him and gave himself for him. You must recognize that God loves you and gave himself for you, too. You must accept his sacrificial death as payment for your sin, the gift of his love. God shows his unconditional love for us by the sacrifice of Christ, and to be saved is to respond to it.

An awareness of Jesus' extreme love for me was the most important element in my own conversion. The morning I was converted was the morning I first recognized that God loved me. Growing up without a father or mother had left me with uncertainty concerning love. And previous to my conversion, as it appears to me looking back on it, one of the driving forces in my life was to gain the approval and certainty of love from others. Yet I could never quite be sure that I was loved—until the morning I gave my life to Christ. I knew then that there was a heavenly Father who loved me, and my natural response was to return that love.

I see this as the essence of Christianity—that human beings should attempt to return God's love by a life of obedience and service to him. The Bible says that the important thing is "not that we loved God, but that he loved us and sent his Son as an atoning sacrifice for our sins" (1 John 4:10). Paul says in Philippians that the goal of his life was "to know Christ and the power of his resurrection and the fellowship of sharing in his sufferings" (3:10). Clearly, much of Paul's motivation came from recognizing the goodness of God and desiring to return God's love with a life of service. This should be a minimal mission statement for all Christians.

The Christian and the Mind of Christ

When Paul says in Philippians 2:5, "Your attitude should be the same as that of Christ Jesus," the first thing he follows it by is the teaching that Christ was a servant. He had a servant's mind, having come to serve others rather than himself. Similarly, the prophet Isaiah described the Messiah as the "suffering Servant." Mark says, "For even the Son of Man did not come to be served, but to serve, and to give his life as a ransom for many" (Mark 10:45).

Modern Christianity frightens me. We tend to believe that God should serve us and meet our needs. Indeed, we tend to measure his love by how much he meets our needs or, better yet, our wants. We have reversed the roles and have turned our mission upside down so that God's blessings have become material possessions or financial prosperity. What we call "Christianity" is often only an extension of our own individualism and greed. Only the Bible can set us straight and help us see clearly that our purpose on earth is to "love the Lord [our] God with all [our] heart and with all [our] soul and with all [our] strength" and to "love [our] neighbor as [ourselves]" (Deuteronomy 6:5; Leviticus 19:18; cf. Matthew 22:34-40). This leaves no room for a "me" God or for living a "me"-type Christianity. Jesus was a servant.

Genesis 24 provides a great example of what that means. Abraham had sent his servant back to his homeland to secure a bride for Isaac, and the servant was enthused about his mission. He knew his job well and did it. He never mentions himself—only his master Abraham, and his master's son, Isaac.

His commitment to Abraham also meant that his needs would be met, for he shared the wealth of his master. This gave him a freedom to share the concerns of his master only, rather than his own needs.

Jesus said, "If anyone would come after me, he must deny himself and take up his cross and follow me" (Matthew 16:24). This is not an abandonment of one's self, but rather confidently putting one's self into the hands of the God who created us, knows us completely, and loves us.

In Matthew 6:33, Jesus said, "Seek first [God's] kingdom and his righteousness, and all these things will be given to you as well." Again, this is a promise of God's provision for his own. We cannot properly use this to justify our selfish, individualistic ways. It is wrong to allow greed to be our purpose for seeking God's kingdom.

Three years after my conversion, I found myself back in Mississippi in a little town called Mendenhall. I moved in across the tracks and saw firsthand the problems found in any major ghetto in this nation: girls pregnant by the age of fourteen or fifteen, boys with no skills or motivation dropping out of school, unemployment. Success in that little town was to leave—to go to Chicago or Los Angeles—and never come back. Indigenous leadership development was the key, and creative Christian community development became my task.

God gave my wife and me a ministry in the high schools of a five county area. We would lead weekly chapel services. We rented a small storefront building where I would study and prepare my Bible lessons. As we sought God and lived in the midst of these problems, I began to understand how the love of God made visible in Jesus had lost its power. This precious gospel that was supposed to burn through social, economic, racial, and cultural barriers—this gospel that was intended to call us out of the world into a vital relationship with Jesus Christ and each other—was not working. The world was supposed to know of Christ through our love for each other, but it was not learning about him. We had taken that precious and vital gospel message, put it into our own racial and cultural context and had destroyed its very purpose. We had a "form of godliness" but without the power (2 Timothy 3:5). I didn't want to preach that kind of gospel.

Where Should the Servant Serve?

Our mentor, Jesus Christ, began his ministry in the synagogue in Nazareth. He opened the scroll of Isaiah to chapter 61 and began to exalt the afflicted in society:

> "The Spirit of the Lord is on me,
>   because he has anointed me
>   to preach good news to the poor.
> He has sent me to proclaim freedom for the prisoners
>   and recovery of sight for the blind,
>   to release the oppressed,
>   to proclaim the year of the Lord's favor."
> (Luke 4:18-19)

This shows us that Christ's mind moves toward others, especially the poor. His special anointing by the Holy Spirit was to preach the gospel to the poor. As Christ's followers and servants, we have been anointed to follow in Christ's footsteps and preach the gospel to the poor also.

Whenever I get on the subject of preaching to the poor, there are always those who ask, "But what about the rich?" Our instinct is to feel bad because the rich are neglected, although many of us never feel a thing when the majority of the population, the poor, are neglected. Of course, the rich already have their servants, maids, and gardeners; they seem to be much easier to serve. Serving the poor brings many complications and problems. The poor take so much more time and energy, and there is little pay-back or even appreciation in return. The rich have many friends, the poor few.

So what about the rich?

Jesus had a unique and very effective way to reach them. Basically he shared the gospel with the poor and underprivileged, knowing that the rich would hear that something good was happening in town and would therefore seek him out. Jesus would then love them also and draw them into his mission to the poor. Examples include: Zacchaeus, who climbed a tree to see Jesus and ended up paying back four times the amount he had taken from the poor; Matthew, the tax collector, who left all to become a disciple; Nicodemus, who came by night to search for Jesus; and Joseph of Arimathea, who gave his own tomb for Christ's burial. I am convinced that if you work for the poor, the rich will find you, just as the rich found Jesus. They will begin to hang around, share your cause, and find their own avenue for service in return.

It has always been difficult for the poor to acquire the resources needed to find Christ. Hundreds of hungry, illiterate and sick persons are dying daily in places like India and Africa without the saving knowledge of Christ. They do not have the wherewithal to go where the gospel is being preached. We must go to them. The rich find themselves in a different situation, since for them resources are available.

What does this indicate about where we should serve?

Jesus did, indeed, love the rich, just as he loved the poor. But his strategy to spread the good news was such as to reach both segments of society. Some in both segments accepted; some did not.

The rich young ruler found Jesus and wanted to know how he could have joy and fulfillment in life. Jesus told him to give his possessions to the poor. Jesus didn't ask him personally for his money; he told him to give it to the poor and then come back and be his disciple. The opportunity was given, but it was rejected. Jesus did spend time with the rich, but he enlisted them as he "moved" toward the poor. I conclude that obedience to God includes pitching our tents towards the poor in society.

Jesus informs us in Matthew 25:34-45 that the great question to be asked of us at judgment will be: "What about the poor?"

"Then the King will say to those on his right, 'Come, you who are blessed by my Father; take your inheritance, the kingdom prepared for you since the creation of the world. For I was hungry and you gave me something to eat, I was thirsty and you gave me something to drink, I was a stranger and you invited me in, I needed clothes and you clothed me, I was sick and you looked after me, I was in prison and you came to visit me.'

"Then the righteous will answer him, 'Lord, when did we see you hungry and feed you, or thirsty and give you something to drink? When did we see you a stranger and invite you in, or needing clothes and clothe you? When did we see you sick or in prison and go to visit you?'

"The King will reply, 'I tell you the truth, whatever you did for one of the least of these brothers of mine, you did for me'" (vv. 34-40).

To say that the church's mission is to share the gospel with those in need will bring wrath and anger from those who want an easy, convenient gospel. It is what eventually hung Jesus on the cross and fulfilled God's plan of redemption.

James explains it another way:

My brothers, as believers in our glorious Lord Jesus Christ, don't show favoritism. Suppose a man comes into your meeting wearing a gold ring and fine clothes, and a poor man in shabby clothes also comes in. If you show special attention to the man wearing fine clothes and say, "Here's a good seat for you," but say to the poor man, "You stand there" or "Sit on the floor by my feet," have you not discriminated among yourselves and become judges with evil thoughts?

Listen, my dear brothers: Has not God chosen those who are poor in the eyes of the world to be rich in faith and to inherit the kingdom he promised those who love him? But you have insulted the poor. Is it not the rich who are exploiting you? Are they not the ones who are dragging you into court? Are they not the ones who are slandering the noble name of him to whom you belong?

If you really keep the royal law found in Scripture, "Love your neighbor as yourself," you are doing right (James 2:1-8).

There are not many positive things said about the rich in the Bible. In fact, the best thing God says to the rich is that they should help the poor. Even in Mary's beautiful "Magnificat," recorded in Luke 1, it is said that God exalts those of low estate and sends the rich away empty-handed.

"He has performed mighty deeds with his arm;
    he has scattered those who are proud in their
        inmost thoughts.
He has brought down rulers from their thrones
    but has lifted up the humble.
He has filled the hungry with good things
    but has sent the rich away empty" (vv. 51-53).

All people are welcome to come to Jesus, of course. He does not want anyone to perish (2 Peter 3:9). But we must all come to Jesus with a humble, servant attitude and in obedience, and this will result ultimately in our giving attention to the broken, hurting, despised, and neglected in society.

Across the street from our mission in Mendenhall, there lived a little boy about twelve years old who was healing from a terrible burn accident with a tractor. Every day he would visit me, and I began to share with him what I was doing. He watched me prepare my lessons, followed me home for dinner, and hung around my family. Soon he was converted and accepted Christ. He finished high school, and we supported him for fourteen years as he went to Washington Bible College, graduated, and then planted a church in a nearby black community. In 1973, he returned to Mendenhall to take over the ministry we had begun, and he is there today.

Today, in that little poverty-stricken community, there is a health center where blacks and whites can get good medical treatment—together and with dignity. There is a Christian school (grades K-6) serving about two hundred students—and a waiting list. There is a legal clinic to serve the poor and disenfranchised. There is a farm to grow vegetables for an economic base and a thrift store owned by the ministry. It is the largest facility in the town. Leadership development and justice are happening as the youth go to college and come back home to use their skills, serve their people, and take responsibility for their lives.

Justice: What Is It?

"Justice" is basically treating people fairly. It is righteousness, and it is loving our neighbors as ourselves. Justice is an economic issue, understanding who owns what. It is how God's abundant resources are distributed and used, how we use God's earth and land for the highest good of humanity. To understand justice is to understand who owns the earth. Who does own it? Psalm 24:1 says, "The earth is the LORD's, and everything in it, the world, and all who live in it."

To be workers for justice is to be workers with God and his creation. Justice is not equalizing the wealth, but it is giving all mankind an opportunity to share in the benefits of God's creation.

Leviticus 25 lays the foundation for biblical justice. The sabbatical concept was to give everyone a new chance every fifty years. The "Year of Jubilee" was the year of reconciliation; it was the opportunity to have a new lease on life.

How Does One Work for Justice?

We work for justice by helping the poor to know and understand this good God of creation, by assisting them in finding opportunities to work with their own hands, by affirming their dignity and worth, and by them then being able to raise their hands in praise of this good God, our Provider. Justice is having a sabbath—a time to rest from our labor and commune with God.

It has always been God's intention for humanity to work. That is part of what it means to be made in the image of God. I would like to see the Humphrey-Hawkins bill for full employment implemented in our society. With the exception of those unable to work, our high unemployment statistics are one of the greatest tragedies in America. Recent reports tell us there is a 7 percent unemployment rate in this nation. That is bad enough, but it is 15 percent for black people and 40 percent for black teenagers. In many ghettos of our nation, welfare has replaced employment. Something must be done to replace this dehumanizing system with a method that creatively guarantees work. Even though they need our help, the poor must take responsibility for their own destiny and work together with God's help to better our society.

In 1976, I went to Wheaton College to speak in a chapel service for the student body. I shared some things about the desperate conditions in the black community, and I challenged the students to think of missions in the ghettos of our nation. Most were not very much moved by my message, because racism had made them believe they could not share the gospel among blacks here at home.

One young white man, Wayne Gordon, took up my challenge. When he graduated he moved into the community of Lawndale, a section of Chicago recently written about in the book, *The American Millstone*. Lawndale is the worst ghetto in America today.

Wayne moved into this community, got a job in one of the black schools coaching wrestling, started meeting with some of the kids after school and soon founded the Lawndale Community Bible Church. He went back to Wheaton to marry his college sweetheart, a beautiful young white girl, and he brought her back into the community with him. All their wedding gifts were stolen the first night they were in their new apartment, and they have since been robbed at least twelve times. But today, in that community, there is a growing church, a development corporation providing housing, a health center serving the community residents, a youth discipleship program and much more.

Last year, Wayne had eighteen young people from that community away in colleges or universities preparing to come back to Lawndale with their skills and Christian commitments. One lady has graduated from the Yale University School of Medicine. She finished her internship and is now working in the Lawndale clinic as a black physician. Another graduated from Northwestern University and is back in Lawndale directing the educational program. Several years of creative Christian community development will bring more results than many years of welfare dependency.

It is also happening in Poughkeepsie, New York, where another young white man moved into the black ghetto. He started a Bible study because he didn't know what else to do. He heard about our program in Jackson, Mississippi, and brought eight of the black boys from his Bible study to visit one summer. Today one of those eight boys, Bob Watson, is leading a Harambee Learning Center in Poughkeepsie that is one of the most outstanding models of Christian community development anywhere in the country. Currently, they are putting together an innovative day care center to assist teen mothers and fathers to take responsibility for their families, training them to be good parents, and providing a much needed service. A model of biblical justice can be seen in Poughkeepsie, New York.

How Is Justice Implemented?

The answer can be found in what I call the "Three Rs of Christian Community Development"—relocation, reconciliation, and redistribution. These "Three Rs" come out of nearly thirty years of ministry in my home state of Mississippi.

Relocation. This is done as Christians live as neighbors with the poor and model Christian living daily. Shared needs and friendships become a bridge for communicating the good news of Jesus Christ and working together for better conditions in the community. Restoration means restoring community. It means sending our young people off to college to get skills and training, then encouraging them to return to their neighborhoods to implement their new skills for the betterment of the community. The poverty, ghetto, and drug-ridden areas of our nation must be viewed as mission opportunities.

The breakdown in society starts with the breakdown of the family. The black family, in particular, has almost disintegrated in most ghetto areas in America. Statistics are fearful. Modest facts would say that over half of all black infants born in ghettos in the United States are born out of wedlock; 70 percent of all people living in these ghettos are supported by the welfare system; 90 percent of all juvenile delinquents come from broken or disturbed families. Something must be done quickly if we are to have a stable future.

We must begin with the neighborhood and the community. Not only did man lose a personal relationship with God in the Garden of Eden. He also lost a communal relationship with his surroundings. Man was created to be in relationship with God and with other people. The New Testament church emphasized becoming a part of the family of God. We are to be the community of faith, the "called out ones," who care for and love each other. Our community is to know we are Christians by our love.

In the ghettos of this nation, it is not unusual for there to be as many as seven or eight churches within a block or two of each other, yet having no relationship to that neighborhood. These are high crime areas, but people never see any response from the church. There should be a parish system on which the members of these churches sense a responsibility for the betterment of their community. At least one of these churches needs to see itself as the people of God in that place.

Relocation is incarnation, and suburban Christians must be encouraged to come back into urban areas to lend a helping hand.

Reconciliation. This is the original purpose of the gospel: to restore the broken relationships of men and women to God and to each other. The Bible says, "God was reconciling the world to himself in Christ" (2 Corinthians 5:19) and has given us "the ministry of reconciliation" (v. 18).

During the years of our ministry in Mississippi, it was difficult for me to understand exactly how whites perceived the gospel. In most cases, it seemed that they thought the purpose of the gospel was to make one a Baptist. I have found that the gospel is a little more creative than that. Its purpose is to bring reconciliation to blacks, whites, Jews, and Gentiles across racial, cultural, and economic barriers. The goal is to make people followers of Jesus Christ.

A sad fact among many of today's "fundamental evangelicals" is their tendency toward racial prejudice. The belief that "biblical truth" demands racial purity has been one of the greatest downfalls of the church. This parallels the views of conservative theologians who believe that one must be a Republican in order to be a Christian. Christians need to be in a position from which they can witness to all ideologies— democratic, republican, socialistic, communistic and so on. Through the church, the gospel needs to be that prophetic voice of God witnessing to society that there is a living God who uses his people as agents of his truth here on earth.

One of my frustrations about the crisis in South Africa is that everyone I meet from that country is a born-again Christian. It depicts for me what has happened to us in America. People have their political and biblical beliefs crossed. There are not many Christians in South Africa putting up a big fight against apartheid in that country. Likewise, the Christian evangelicals of the 1960s and 1970s were pretty much silent during the Civil Rights Movement. The ones who were bold enough to speak out were thrust into a different political and biblical category called "liberal."

Thus, oppressed peoples have had to look to "liberals" for support. Many countries, such as the Philippines and

Guatemala, are looking to Communism because they do not have even the necessary liberal support. I am convinced that if we do not believe in reconciliation, we do not have a gospel to preach.

Redistribution. This has to do with finding creative ways to empower people to take responsibility for their situation economically and socially. I am not talking about giving hand-outs but rather with training the young and healthy, our future leaders, to function in their particular society. Redistribution deals with more than money. I do not believe that we should take all the money from the rich and give it to the poor, because I know that, if we did that, the rich would have it back again tomorrow. The rich will always find creative ways to get it from people who do not have the necessary skills to keep it.

Human dignity becomes an important factor when people are not given a chance to make it on their own. This results eventually in people just giving up. Today we have whole generations of people who have given up, and welfare dependence is almost out of control. Useful skills need to be taught. People need to learn how to be electricians, painters, carpenters, janitors, computer technicians, cooks, and much more. We need to establish communities where people can become self-sufficient and provide for themselves.

Conclusion and Summary

A Christian is a follower of Jesus Christ with a servant mentality. He directs his attention towards the poor in society and lives in community with them as they both learn to love God and each other in reconciliation. We must carry out Jesus' command to "love the Lord your God with all your heart and with all your soul and with all your mind" and then to "love your neighbor as yourself." That is what Christianity and living out biblical justice in society are.

Chapter 7

The Christian and the Church

Richard John Neuhaus

"*T*he Christian and the Church" is the topic I have been assigned, and I welcome it. A major theme of this volume is reflected in its title, *Transforming Our World: A Call to Action*. And I suppose that one of the truths I most want to press home is that our efforts to transform the world will be futile—worse than futile—unless our eyes are fixed on that promised transformation of the world in the coming again of our Lord Jesus Christ. Any call to action will be useless unless it begins with and returns to the call to faith.

I want to set forth three propositions: (1) the Christian needs the church to be the church, (2) the world needs the church to be the church, and (3) the church is the church when it is obedient to the gospel. Those propositions may seem obvious. But if you take a serious look at the state of American Christianity, it is clear that they are not obvious to many Christians today.

The Christian and the Church
Fifty years ago "Let the church be the church" was the motto of the ecumenical movement—before it became the old,

creaky, cantankerous thing it is in our time. We need to reclaim
and revive that motto. The bitter lines of division among Christians today are over what the church must *do* in the world. But
renewal—even something worthy of being called a "new Reformation"—might begin, if we would only turn our attention to
what the church ought to be in the world first of all, rather
than to what she must *do*.

Evangelical Christians are commonly accused of having
a weak, sub-biblical understanding of the church. And why
should we even attempt to deny the charge? It is often true.
Neglect of the biblical doctrine of the church—a shortchanging
of the corporate character of Christian existence—is endemic
to Protestantism, most particularly to American Protestantism.
And one reason for it is the individualism which is deeply
entrenched in the American experience. It is both a strength
and a weakness of our culture.

Thomas Jefferson said, "I don't need a church. I am my
own sect." Two hundred years later, a woman named Sheila
told the author of *Habits of the Heart*, "I believe in God. I'm
not a religious fanatic. I can't remember the last time I went
to church, but my faith has carried me a long way. I call it
'Sheilaism,' just my own little voice."

An astonishing 81 percent of Americans say they agree
with the statement: "An individual should arrive at his or her
own religious belief independent of any churches or
synagogues." This seems to me to be far removed from the
words of the One who told us, "Where two or three come
together in my name, there am I with them" (Matthew 18:20).

I saw a church in Toronto which has inscribed on the wall
of its sanctuary: "*He is not here!* He is risen." What a strange
thing to say about the gathering place of his disciples! He *is*
there. And he is *here*. To be sure, he is with us also in our
solitude, one by one. But he has made us for community, and
he has called us to the community that is the church.

Someone may ask, "What do you mean by 'church'?"
That question would be better framed as, "*Who* do we mean
by 'church'?" For the "church" is "the body of Christ," which

is, the apostle tells us, being "built up until we all reach unity in the faith and in the knowledge of the Son of God and become mature, attaining to the whole measure of the fullness of Christ" (Ephesians 4:12, 13). In a profound way, there is no Christian apart from the church, the body of which Christ is head.

"*Hier stehe ich* (Here I stand)," said Martin Luther. That is a certain kind of individualism, a founding sentiment of the Protestant tradition. But Luther uttered those words not as a declaration of defiant individualism, but rather as meaning, "I take my stand with the prophets, evangelists, apostles, and the great cloud of witnesses in the church who have been obedient to the Word of God." Only later would Luther's words be stolen to support the creed of modern individualism. Luther intended not the dissolution of the church, but the reformation of the church. And that is too often forgotten by many who claim the Reformation heritage.

A friend of mine from New York heard that I had been invited to address Congress on the Bible II on "the church." He said, "I hope you'll tell them that the church is God's tool for reforming society." Well, yes and no. The biblical view is not of the church as God's tool, but of the church as God's people. The church is not an instrument to be used but a community to be served. Its purpose is not the achievement of this good or that good but to advance what the *Westminster Shorter Catechism* calls "the chief end of man," namely, "to glorify God and to enjoy him forever."

The church is not for hire, no matter how noble the intentions of those who would hire it. The church is bound *for* the kingdom of God and bound *by* the kingdom of God. To settle for less than the kingdom of God is to be less than the church of Christ. That is the only transformation of the world worthy of the investment of our hope. "To glorify God and enjoy him forever" is the high calling to which we are called, and that high calling is betrayed when we weary of the transcendent promise and turn the church into a tool for feeding our desires, even our most worthy desires, here and now.

In biblical teaching, the church betrayed is Christ

betrayed. Therefore, a Congress on the Bible must also be a congress calling Christians to repentance. The first of Luther's "Ninety-five Theses" nailed to the door of the Castle Church in Wittenberg was, you recall: "When our Lord and Master Jesus Christ says, 'Repent,' he means that the whole life of believers upon earth should be a constant and perpetual repentance."[1]

The Christian needs the church to be a repenting community.

The Christian needs the church to be a zone of truth in a world of mendacity.

The Christian needs the church to be a community in which our sin need not be disguised but can be honestly faced and plainly confessed, because we know that the "worst word" about us as sinners is not the "last word." The "last word" is that we are forgiven sinners, forgiven through the shed blood of Jesus Christ our Lord.

We are emboldened to let the church be the church—a community resounding with the No and the Yes of God's thunderous judgment and immeasurable mercy. This is the living Word that shatters our human pretensions and then, after the shattering, tenderly picks up the broken pieces of our lives and fits them together into the likeness of him who makes all things new. This is the Word of sin and grace, of law and gospel, of judgment and mercy. The church lives from this Word, and it lives for this Word—or it lives not at all. To evoke faith in this Word is the church's reason for existence.

The greatest crisis of our age is not what the editorial writers in the prestige press think it to be. The greatest crisis as we approach the start of the third Christian millennium is not the threat of nuclear war, nor world hunger, nor AIDS, nor the breakdown of the family, nor the desperate plight of the urban black underclass, nor myriad other catastrophes about which we are, or should be, deeply concerned. The greatest crisis of our time, and of every time, is unbelief.

The question before us is the question our Lord asked, as recorded in Luke 18: "When the Son of Man comes, will he find faith on the earth?" (v. 8). After everything is said and done, all our concerns are weighed and all our actions are taken, the great concern of the Lord Jesus Christ will still be: "Will there be faith on the earth?" We must subordinate all our concerns, causes, and agendas to that end if the church is to be the church.

Those who would use the church as a tool are busy about many things. But those who would hold the church to that question have chosen the one thing needful.

Our Lord both relativizes and empowers our efforts to effect change. Our efforts are relativized, because we know that all the changes we can make, or even all the changes that we can envision, are at best penultimate, our hearts being fixed on the ultimate transformation that will be effected by the coming of the kingdom. Our efforts are empowered, because we act, not trusting in our own successes but in his final vindication. We are enabled to act in the courage of our uncertainty, because we do not know what our actions—our most fervent, most devoted, most self-sacrificial actions—will mean in the end. We do not need to know. It is enough that he knows.

We are not paralyzed by the knowledge that we may fail or err either. If we make mistakes in our acting—and we certainly will—God's power to forgive is greater than our capacity to err. And if we fail—as we often will—we can remember that it is from broken pieces that God makes his creation whole. This is the gospel of the cross of Christ. It is a stumbling block to the smugly secure and foolishness to the smugly sophisticated. But to those who believe, it is the power of God unto salvation.

"When the Son of Man comes, will he find faith on the earth?" This is the question that throws into question all programs, causes, campaigns, and concerns of his church on earth. When the church refuses to hold itself accountable to that question it becomes as salt that has lost its savor, and it will surely be—as it deserves to be—despised and trampled under foot by the world.

The World and the Church

This leads to my next point, namely, that the *world* needs the church to be the church. The church is a community ahead of time. It is a community of the end time—in time. We know now, and proclaim now, what one day will be known by all— when every knee shall bow and every tongue confess it— namely, that "Jesus Christ is Lord, to the glory of God the Father" (Philippians 2:11). The church best serves the world when it confesses that, and so is most distinctively and most unapologetically the church.

The World Council of Churches has a motto that says, "The world sets the agenda for the church." I respectfully submit that this is a grave error. The church and its gospel throw into question the agenda of the world—all the agendas of the world— and open the world to possibilities of which it has never dared to dream. No agenda for change, no program— no matter how radical—can compare with the revolution of a people recreated to glorify God and enjoy him forever. When the church dares to be different, it models for the world what God calls the world to become. The church models what it means to be a community of caring and character.

For Christians, what we can *do* is more limited, less interesting and, finally, less important, than what by the grace of God we can *be*.

We have no illusions—or we ought to have no illusions— about our ability to establish the kingdom of God on earth. We do indeed strive to build a world in which the strong are just and power is tempered by mercy, in which the weak are nurtured and the marginal embraced, and those at the entrance gates and those at the exit gates of life are protected both by law and love. We strive for such a world. Indeed, we must strive for such a world, not because success is guaranteed but because love for our neighbor is commanded. And yet, in all of our striving we know, we never forget for a moment, that short of the coming of the kingdom of God, the principalities and powers of the present age will continue to rage and thus make mockery of our striving to produce transformation.

Yet again, we persist in striving—driven not by illusions of success but empowered by a promise. And the promise is that, in the final accounting, nothing done for the love of Christ is done in vain. Through our disappointments, mistakes, and weariness—defying the appearance of futility—comes the word of our Master, "Do not be afraid, little flock, for your Father has been pleased to give you the kingdom" (Luke 12:32). We will not succeed in building the society we desire. But we, the church, will by God's grace be the society that it is our destiny and duty to be.

I have an admittedly eccentric exegesis of our theme passage from Micah: "Act justly . . . love mercy and . . . walk humbly with your God" (6:8). My exegesis goes like this: "Strive to do justice—strive real hard. And when you discover that it is often impossible, then at least love mercy. And when you have lived long enough and failed often enough to realize how hard it is to do justice and even to love mercy all the time, then, brothers and sisters, you will know why it is that you must walk humbly with your God." I say this because the demands of the passage decline from doing justice to loving mercy to walking humbly in order that the grace of God may ascend. Why? Because that is our only reliance—not our capacity to do justice or even to love mercy, since our capacities to do both are limited. When we walk humbly with God, we throw ourselves upon his grace alone.

In contemporary Christianity the word *justice* is much used. That is good. But sometimes it is used too facilely, especially when it is referred to Christian political action. In many of our churches there are valuable peace-and-justice-networks—filled in most cases with wonderful Christian people—which are demanding that the world become the kind of community that, were the truth to be told, we Christians do not dare to be ourselves. Is this right? Isn't it true that the world does not need Christian exhortation so much as it needs Christian people, a Christian example. Christians on the right and on the left of the political spectrum are forever investing their hope in the politics of the moment, forgetting that the only politics worthy of our hope are the genuinely new politics of the heavenly *polis*—the city that comes down from above, the city of God.

The world needs a church that dares to defy the pervasiveness and imperiousness of the political in our world. The great Dr. Samuel Johnson wrote,

> How small a part of all that human hearts endure
> Can laws or kings either cause or cure.

Here we arrive at a paradox, and it is this: the more the church is focused on effecting change in the world, the less effective the church will be in changing the world. The imperiousness of the political! That is not the only form of apostasy in our time, but it is among the most virulent forms of apostasy in our churches.

Liberation theologians of a Marxist stripe (on the left) and conservative theologians of a theonomist stripe (on the right) would create a partisan church. Membership in a partisan church is defined not by the gospel of God's justifying grace in Christ, but by ideology, by political alignment, and by where one stands on the public policy issues of the day. In their extreme forms, ideology and politics are said to *be* the gospel of Jesus Christ. In their more tempered forms, Christians are led to the habit of mind by which they measure the church's mission by its influence on what is ridiculously called "the real world"—meaning, the world of political and social change.

But moderate apostasy is still apostasy. And indeed, this may be its more dangerous form just because it appears so innocent. Its lethal implications are disguised by the appearance of moderation.

This apostasy means that in many of our churches, God's people hunger for the bread of life and are too often given stones borrowed from the deadly power games of the world.

Preachers become influence peddlers, and churches are turned into political lobbies which, no matter how successful or how much clout they think they have, are in fact pitiful appendages to agendas that are set in the public arena by people who neither understand nor care about the nature or mission of the church of Jesus Christ.

The church as a tool is a church of fools. The apostle writes, "You foolish [Americans]! Who has bewitched you? Before your very eyes Jesus Christ was clearly portrayed as crucified. I would like to learn just one thing from you: Did you receive the Spirit by [works of social transformation], or by believing what you heard?" (cf. Galatians 3:1-2).

Of course, Christians should be engaged in the public square. More and more Christians need to be told that—more and more persuasively, more and more urgently. Christians need to be engaged in the public square relentlessly, audaciously, defiantly, sometimes even confrontationally, if that is required to get the necessary conversation going. The ministry of the church, however, is to equip the saints for their vocations in the world, and political action is not a large part—indeed, it is not necessarily even any part—of every Christian's vocation. There are many—children, the aged, the mentally ill, those who believe they have found better ways of loving their neighbors—all of whom are not less a part of the church simply because they are apolitical. The church's vocation is to sustain many different vocations. And it is to keep those who are politically engaged engaged with one another, especially when they are politically opposed. They are to be engaged with one another not only within the bond of civility but, much more importantly, within the bond of the love of Christ.

The truth of the gospel transcends our disagreements about all lesser truths. And it is by that truth that we are knit together in mutual dependence and accountability. By that truth, the church is enabled to be a zone of truth in a world of impassioned mendacities—not least of all in the world of impassioned political mendacities. Not to class struggle, nor to programs of liberal reform, nor to campaigns for traditional values, nor to the crusade for Christian America—to none of these is the kingdom of God promised, but to the little flock of those who walk humbly with their God because they know they walk by grace and not by works. That is the gospel.

Of that gospel the apostle Paul declares, "Even if we or an angel from heaven should preach a gospel other than the one we preached to you, let him be eternally condemned" (Galatians 1:8). Those are hard words required by a hard truth. But the hard truth today is that in our time, as then, other gospels are being preached. And in much of the church, these other gospels have displaced the gospel of God's justification of the godless by grace through faith. There are "therapeutic" gospels, "get-rich" gospels, gospels of "material fulfillment," of "nationalistic hubris," of "revolutionary utopias." We are awash in other gospels.

It is not too much to say (indeed, it is necessary to say) that the gospel of Jesus Christ is as thoroughly eclipsed today— eclipsed by prescriptions of what the reformers called "works righteousness"—as it was in the Christianity of the sixteenth century, except that now works righteousness is built not upon pilgrimages and the relics of the saints but upon politics and the rule of the just. Four hundred and seventy years have gone by, and John Tetzel is alive and well and doing a booming business in America—not least among those who claim to be the heirs of the Reformation.

Obedience to the Gospel

The Christian needs the church to be the church. The world needs the church to be the church. My final point, a brief one, is that the church is the church when it is obedient to the gospel.

To an ominous degree in America, the church is not obedient to the gospel. *We* are not obedient to the gospel. Luther had it right, I believe. And something like a new Reformation might get underway if we were to take to thousands of churches, perhaps even nailing it to their doors, this profound biblical truth: "When our Lord and Master Jesus Christ says, 'Repent,' he means that the whole life of believers upon earth should be a constant and perpetual repentance."

Chapter 7, Notes

1. J. H. Merle D'Aubigne, *The Life and Times of Martin Luther* (Chicago: Moody Press, 1958), 110.

PART 3

ANSWERING THE CALL

Chapter 8

Christian Responsibility and Public Life

Senator William Armstrong

S ome time ago, my wife Ellen and I traveled overseas to a country that some of you may also have visited. It is a country which has made great material progress in recent years, yet remains desperately poor. It observes the forms of democracy but does so in a way that makes human freedom a mockery. In this country neighbors spy upon neighbors. People are always looking over their shoulder to see if the secret police are observing.

While we were there we met some men and women we will never forget. One was a man by the name of Zelichenok. He was arrested shortly after we chatted with him in his apartment in Leningrad. I do not know exactly what he was accused of having done, but I do know that he had offended the regime by asking to leave the country in order to practice his faith freely. He is just one of millions around the world who suffer such oppression.

At midnight, with the KGB in the car behind, we visited a lady in Leningrad whose husband is a Baptist minister. He was not there. As a matter of fact, he was behind barbed wire, serving the third year of a five-year prison sentence for the crime of preaching the gospel. I was extraordinarily impressed with this woman, because she was not bitter or angry. She gave every appearance of being completely composed as she explained that she harbored no resentment. "The policemen were only doing their job," she said, "just as my husband was." God had called him to tell people about Jesus Christ.

We met a woman whose sister had been arrested and had served a jail term for the crime of copying the Bible on the typewriter.

We visited another person by the name of Andre Kistyokovsky. We had been sent to see him by Mrs. Aleksandr Solzhenitsyn, who had heard that we were going to Russia and thought that if we would call on Mr. Kistyokovsky, that expression of interest by persons from the outside might afford him a degree of protection. He had undertaken a very dangerous project by the standards of that country. He had agreed to head up the so-called "Solzhenitsyn Fund"—established with the proceeds of that great author's writings—for the relief of widows, wives, orphans, and elderly parents of persons who have been jailed. The day he announced that he was accepting this assignment, the KGB came to call on him, hauled him down to the police station, told him he was getting mixed up in something which was treason, ransacked his home and took his typewriter. In fact, when we visited him he was attempting to do his translation work with a pencil.

I marveled at the composure of this man. We sat in his tiny apartment, practically speaking into the chandelier, believing that somewhere there was a microphone hidden and that what we were saying was being overheard. I wondered how in the face of that kind of tension and pressure he could maintain such tremendous composure, knowing that sooner or later he would be sent to prison if, indeed, something worse did not happen to him. But he revealed the secret of his poise. He told us that he had become a Christian and had recently been baptized. What a step of faith in a place like that!

Well, we came home and said something that I suppose we always say when we have been traveling abroad. But we said it with new meaning, significance and understanding. "God bless America!" This really is a nation beautiful "for spacious skies and amber waves of grain." And God really has "shed his grace" on the United States of America. There has never been a country like it. There has never been a nation with so much freedom.

In many countries around the world Christians are not able to meet openly to talk about the Bible and spiritual matters. They have to meet in secret. Or if they do meet openly, it is at great risk to those who participate. Someone will be standing at the door to take names and identify people. And the next day they will find that they have lost their jobs, or they will be discriminated against or harassed in some other way.

We are free to meet, free to worship, speak, publish, travel. We have freedom of opportunity. We have much that is utterly unknown in many, many countries around the world. Eight out of ten people on this planet live in conditions of slavery or under circumstances that are far less than completely free. There has never been a country with such tremendous material prosperity. Even poor people here enjoy a standard of living and affluence beyond the dreams of people in many parts of the globe.

Did it ever occur to you to wonder why? Do you suppose it is because God loves us more than other people? I do not think so.

But there *is* something unique about the United States of America—not that God loves us better, not that he has singled us out for special treatment—but rather that among believers, and even among nonbelievers, there has been what *Time* called "a strain of righteousness" that lies deep in our character.

John Gunther wrote, "Ours is the only country deliberately founded on a good idea, an idea which combines a commitment to man's inalienable rights and a belief in an ultimate moral right—and sinful man's obligation to do good." From this biblical consensus, from what men and women at the time of the founding of our republic knew from reading the Bible, came the articles of our national faith—the Declaration of Independence and our Constitution—both embodying extraordinary concern for the rights of accused persons, for religious liberty and for human freedom. In turn, from these political arrangements have come all of our national power and tremendous prosperity—unlike anything seen in the world before.

More than a century ago, a great French statesman and author came to this country. His name was Alexis de Tocqueville. He traveled throughout our land and wrote a report on our country, which stands as a monument to his insight and perspicacity. He said,

> I sought for the greatness and genius of America in her commodious harbors and ample rivers, and it was not there; in her fertile fields and boundless forests, and it was not there; in her rich mines and vast world commerce, and it was not there; in her democratic Congress and her matchless Constitution, and it was not there. Not until I went into the churches of America and heard their pulpits aflame with righteousness did I understand the secret of her genius and power. America is great because she is good. And if America ever ceases to be good, America will cease to be great.

The United States Today

Would a perceptive observer come to our country and write such a report today? I think not.

A report of an entirely different character appeared in the *Washington Post* recently. It was a huge article that dominated the front page and some of the inside pages of this great newspaper. It did not make pleasant reading for practicing politicians and others in my line of work, because in five days of door-to-door canvassing the reporters for this paper found voters and community leaders strikingly negative about the direction our country has been taking and particularly about the performance of people in positions of national leadership. The people polled were cynical, disillusioned, and pessimistic. One man summed it up by saying, "You can't trust anybody. It is a sickening way to feel." Voters said that things are slipping out of control. They feel manipulated and distrustful. They said they believed politicians would do and say just about anything to get elected and re-elected.

I hate to admit it, but they are pretty close to the mark.

What the *Washington Post* story did not say—though it may well have—is that this attitude of disillusionment is not directed only toward people in political life. It is also becoming increasingly common in reference to the other institutions of our society.

Our faith in the fairness of the stock market has been rocked this summer by disclosures of stock market rigging and insider trading. We are disgusted and saddened by what has happened at PTL. Sexual misconduct, abuse of power, and the mishandling of funds would be a scandal in any organization, but they are tragic in an organization dedicated to the glory of God. Sports figures, heroes to our young people, throw away their lives in pursuit of the thrills induced by drugs. Smut has become a multi-billion-dollar industry. And whether you believe that AIDS is a public health problem or a moral issue, there can be no denying that it is looming as the greatest menace of its kind since the fourteenth century.

A noted educator and author of this year's hottest bestseller of its kind, *The Closing of the American Mind*, recently wrote a newspaper article in which he said something profoundly important about what is happening in our country. He asked, "Is rock music rotting the minds of our children?" He answered, "Yes."

Adultery has become so commonplace that when a candidate for president of the United States recently was forced from the race because of allegations of such misconduct, many people in this country thought he was getting a raw deal. And, believe it or not, a person who had been the nominee of a major party for vice-president of the United States (who nearly became vice-president of the United States and who might therefore have become president of the United States) responded to what happened by saying, "Personal values and moral character of presidential candidates are irrelevant and unimportant."

How far have we come in this country? This summer another member of the United States House of Representatives announced his homosexuality. The reaction of the press was, "So what?"

In our generation there are or will be 47 million divorces, 550,000 deaths from drunk driving, 23 million users of illegal drugs, 18 million abortions, 189 million serious crimes, and 366,000 murders. Well over half of all employees cheat their employers, according to a recent survey. More than ten billion dollars is spent on sex magazines, sexually explicit movies and video tapes.

Our children are the first children since the Mayflower who cannot read as well as or better than their parents. And suicide has become a leading cause of death among teenagers.

Is it any wonder that a recent nationwide poll found 67 percent of the people in this country saying that things are heading seriously in the wrong direction?

Denver's new archbishop, J. Francis Stafford, held a news conference not long ago to warn that our constitutional system will decay unless civic virtue is nurtured and celebrated. "Character is the fundamental issue," he said. Today Americans are in the grip of what he termed, "debonair nihilism" fed by moral decay in business, politics, religion, and private lives.

What we are seeing is the breakdown of standards of character and integrity, which the people who founded this country took for granted. We are living out the logical and inevitable consequences of a desire by our country to enjoy the benefits of its heritage while denying its validity. Francis Schaeffer put it well when he said that we are "living in the memory of our Christian consensus." We have become what somebody called "a nation of spiritual coupon-clippers, living on the investment of an earlier generation."

Living on the Memory

In my judgment that is the reason why millions of abortions are taking innocent lives and why the federal government continues to grant favorable tax status to organizations which provide facilities for and perform abortions. Surely God is calling us to stand with men like Senators Gordon Humphrey and Jessie Helms and others who are seeking repeal of such an unfair tax provision.

It is appalling to contemplate that Hugh Hefner, the publisher of *Playboy* magazine, has been given a prestigious award by one of the nation's foremost civil rights organizations, and that Bob Guccione, the publisher of *Penthouse* magazine, was recently named "Publisher of the Year" by the Periodical and Book Association of America.

But I am going to tell you something. Long after the names of Hefner and Guccione are forgotten, history will recall the faithfulness of Florida businessman Jack Eckerd who, against the advice of his business associates and risking millions of dollars in sales and profits, banned such publications from his drugstores across Florida—provoking the conscience of other businessmen and businesswomen who have followed suit.

Now that Seven-Eleven, Hi's Dairy Stores and one of the large truck-stop operators have decided to stop selling these magazines, it may be that the United States government is the largest distributor of such magazines in the world, giving tacit approval to the ideas, concepts, values, and lifestyles that they advocate by permitting the sale of such publications in literally hundreds of government office buildings, PXs and embassies around the world. Surely God is calling us to pray for and stand with the men and women who are calling on President Reagan to issue an executive order forbidding the sale of such publications in government locations.

It is discouraging when the singers of dirty lyrics and those who portray, sing, and perform music which glorifies Satan worship are welcomed in respectable, even prestigious gatherings. That, too, is happening day after day. But coura- geous men like the former president of CBS, Arthur Taylor, and godly women like Tipper Gore and Susan Baker, are think- ing, writing, and organizing to turn the tide. I believe God is calling us to pray for them and help them with their task.

PTL is going through the wringer. Because this scandal is so public there are going to be a lot of people who will see what is happening and have an excuse to say, "Christian minis- tries are all the same; they are all corrupt." They are going to give up on television evangelism, and perhaps other Christian works as well. I believe that God is calling on us to say straight out, "They are not all the same. There are organizations which are scrupulously honest in the handling of their funds, which send us audited financial statements and whose leaders serve sacrificially. They deserve our support." I believe God is calling us to make such a statement.

We have not heard the last of the scandals on Wall Street. We are going to hear of more wrongdoing. But I believe God is calling on us to stand shoulder to shoulder with investment bankers like Burt Sorensen and brokers like Ed Britton, who are drawing men and women in the investment industry to Jesus Christ. In fact, I am convinced God is challenging us to be the light in every dark area of life—in business, politics, the arts, the professions, journalism, international relations, in the prisons, schools, work places, homes, and churches all over this country.

I do not think we are only talking about some kind of marginal adjustment in American attitudes. It is far too late to start fine-tuning the American psyche. I do not think Ruth Graham was wrong when she said that if God does not judge the United States of America soon, he is going to owe an apology to Sodom and Gomorrah.

Habits of the Heart

Can we expect the government to solve this problem for us? Will the president do it? Will Congress do it? I do not think so. I have devoted many years to personal service in government. I believe it to be worthy; I think it is important. I am thankful that many good people are called to that service. And there is an important, even a strategic role for people in public life to play. But, you know, after these years in Congress, after having voted on thousands of bills and even after having seen some of my own enacted into law, I am convinced that the crucial issue is not our laws but rather our thought-life as a nation—what de Tocqueville called "the habits of our heart."

The distinguished author Russell Kirk has identified three groups of ideas or principles which, he says, inevitably and invisibly control any people, whether they are the bushmen of Australia or those living in a modern industrial society. "The most important of these principles," he said, "is the set of moral convictions which a people hold: their ideas about the relationship between God and man, about virtue and vice, honesty and dishonesty, honor and dishonor." This brings me back to where we began. The reason this country has been blessed is because it was founded on the Bible. The Bible, the holy Word of God, is the basis of this country.

Not long ago, we celebrated the two hundredth anniversary of the Constitution of the United States, one of the most remarkable documents in human history. We are justifiably proud of it. But many historians believe, as a matter of scholarship, that the Bible—perhaps even more than the Constitution of the United States—is truly our founding document, the source of the uniqueness of the American republic. The very minds of the people who wrote the Constitution of the United States rang with the cadences of the Bible. Our greatest national leaders have quoted the Bible.

President Andrew Jackson said, "The Bible is the rock upon which our republic rests." Abraham Lincoln said, "The Bible is the greatest gift God ever gave to man." President Eisenhower said, "Our civilization is built on its words." George Washington forthrightly declared, "It is impossible to rightly govern without God and the Bible." The Ten Commandments hang above the head of the Chief Justice of the United States Supreme Court.

America is the land of the Bible.

I am convinced that only the Bible can provide the ultimate standard, the benchmark, by which we may hold our public policy and our political leaders accountable. It is the only standard that has the authority, relevance, precision, and power by which we may reform the thought-life of this country.

The world says, "Blessed is the nation whose Gross National Product is rising 4 percent or more after inflation." Jesus says, "Blessed are those who hunger and thirst for righteousness" (Matthew 5:6).

The world says, "A booming stock market is good for a nation." The Bible says, "Righteousness exalts a nation" (Proverbs 14:34).

The world is at war. Jesus Christ says, "Peace I leave with you; my peace I give you" (John 14:27).

The world is addicted to materialism, hedonism, and idolatry. Jesus Christ says, "I am the way and the truth and the life" (John 14:6).

Imagine the potential of a world at peace, a world in which men and women could live together in the relationship of a loving family as brothers and sisters—no one trying to take advantage of anyone else, but just trying to serve one another. The world says, "This is impossible." Jesus Christ says, "I have overcome the world" (John 16:33).

What is the battle plan if we are serious about doing something to combat pornography, drugs, abortion, and low ethics in high places? The plan is in the Bible.

Let us hold unswervingly to the hope we profess, for he who promised is faithful. And let us consider how we may spur one another on toward love and good deeds. Let us not give up meeting together, as some are in the habit of doing, but let us encourage one another—and all the more as you see the Day approaching (Hebrews 10:23-25).

Chapter 9

The Kingdom of God and Human Kingdoms

Charles W. Colson

*I*t is impossible to read the preceding chapters without coming to the conclusion that we live in a period of enormous disillusionment, what *Time* magazine called a "moral morass."

So I start from that point and ask two questions: (1) Why are we in the situation our country and civilization are in? and (2) What role do you and I, as individuals and as representatives of the church of Jesus Christ, have in beginning to work our society out of it?

To understand our current dilemma one must go back in history. I would like to take you to a dramatic and decisive moment in modern history: 2 September 1945. In that year the world had emerged, bloodied and weary, from a most horrendous war—six years of ravage and bloodshed, often teetering on the brink of catastrophe. Now, on this momentous day, the sun climbed high over Tokyo Bay and the steel decks of the great battleship, the USS Missouri, grew hot. General Douglas MacArthur stood with representatives of the allied powers to receive the formal surrender of Japan. In the center of the rows of khaki, medals, and ribbons stood a microphone, an old mess table covered with green felt, and two straight chairs. High above, the stars and stripes furled in the breeze—the same flag that had hung over the Capitol building on 7 December 1941, the day the Japanese had attacked Pearl Harbor.

At precisely 9:00 A.M. eleven Japanese officials wearing silk hats, ascots and cutaways climbed the stairway of the ship, their faces devoid of expression. MacArthur, wearing his familiar sunglasses and visored cap, walked to the microphone. He stood erect and confident, though his hand trembled slightly as he held the sheet of notes before him:

> We are gathered here, representatives of the major warring powers, to conclude a solemn agreement whereby peace may be restored. . . . It is my earnest hope, and indeed the hope of all mankind, that from this solemn occasion a better world shall emerge . . . a world founded upon faith and understanding, a world dedicated to the dignity of man and the fulfillment of his most cherished wish—for freedom, tolerance and justice.

At eight minutes past nine, MacArthur sat at the table and signed the surrender agreement. Overhead was a glorious aerial pageant—four hundred B-29s and fifteen hundred carrier planes swept across the sky with a deafening roar. World War II was over! MacArthur then strode again to the microphone and spoke the first words of peace to a waiting world:

> Today the guns are silent. A great tragedy has ended. A great victory has been won. The skies no longer rain death—the seas bear only commerce—men everywhere walk upright in the sunlight. The entire world is quietly at peace. . . . Men since the beginning of time have sought peace, but military alliances, balances of power, leagues of nations, all in turn failed, leaving the only path to be by the crucible of war. . . . We have had our last chance. If we do not now devise some greater and more equitable system, Armageddon will be at our door.

The problem basically is theological and involves a spiritual recrudescence and improvement of human character. . . . It must be of the spirit if we are to save the flesh."[1]

The year 1945, "Year Zero," as one historian has called it. MacArthur told a weary world that hung on each word that, if there was hope for mankind, it was in the realm of the spirit that we must be saved. I think that may have been the most prophetic sermon of the twentieth century—delivered by a layman on board the USS Missouri in Tokyo Bay.

A Land without Values

But what was the response? In the postwar euphoria, with the veterans ready to come home, take the G.I. Bill, go to school, buy a home and have babies, MacArthur's words were soon forgotten. Times were good: the nation had a nuclear monopoly; business boomed. Eisenhower's 1956 re-election theme, "Peace, Progress and Prosperity," captured the mood of the nation.

The 1960s began with the same confidence. But soon that confidence was shaken to its foundations by a rapid-fire series of events. John Kennedy, Robert Kennedy, and Martin Luther King were assassinated. Streets across the nation reeked of pot and tear gas as a new generation, whose rebellion was fueled by existential writers, did drugs and dodged the draft. "Do your own thing," became the password.

In the 1970s came the "me" decade—yuppyism, materialism, and a loss of a sense of community.

And in the 1980s we are reaping the consequences of trying to get along without any values at all. We have inherited what Richard Neuhaus has called the "naked public square."

What happened? What happened is that the idea of truth itself has been relativized so that there are no absolute rights or wrongs anymore in public discourse. The twentieth century has been seized by the powerful ideas of an odd prophet—a syphilitic and eventually insane German by the name of Friedrich Nietzsche. In 1889, Nietzsche wrote, "God is dead." But these were not the ramblings of a village atheist. Many before him had denied God's existence. Nietzsche's point was not that God does not exist, but rather that man has killed God. We live *as if* God does not exist. We have families, educate our children, form governments, make war—all *as if* there is no God. Thus, God is dead because we have killed him.

Nietzsche predicted that this would lead to the destruction of the very idea of good and evil. There would be wars, he believed, of a kind that could never have happened on the earth before, because there would be no transcendent guide to steady our steps, no right or wrong. People would seek to impose their will on others by sheer power. No abiding principle would remain by which we could logically prefer "all men are created equal" to "the weak to the wall."

The French theologian, mathematician and philosopher of some centuries ago, Blaise Pascal, said that when men are separated from God there are only two options. The first is that they will begin to imagine they are gods themselves. That is what is happening in the 40 percent of the world that is dominated by Marxism today. Man's will to power, believing he is his own god, has set itself up in the place of God while suppressing and persecuting true religion.

The second option is that men will seek satisfaction in their senses. Allan Bloom, author of that masterful work *The Closing of the American Mind*, has said, describing today's culture, "The self has become the modern substitute for the soul."[2] We seek meaning through ourselves. But paradoxically, one can never find meaning through oneself. I know. I sought it for forty years and found this choice to be empty. A person can only find meaning when he or she dies to self and finds the risen Christ. There is no other meaning. Yet our entire culture persists in the hopeless search for meaning through self.

A recent study by sociologist Robert Bellah, entitled *Habits of the Heart*, examines modern values. Bellah interviewed a number of people to determine their deepest motivations. When they were asked about work and its meaning, most defined it in terms of personal advancement. When they were asked about marriage, they defined it in terms of personal development. And when they were asked about the church, they defined it in terms of personal fulfillment. It was all self. Self has replaced the soul.

Let me illustrate what this has brought us to. Last November at Harvard University there was a nationwide conference of educators. They were discussing reforms in higher education. In the midst of this discussion Cornell University President Frank Rhodes said, "Perhaps it is time that we gave real and sustained attention to students' intellectual and moral well-being." Suddenly there were gasps, followed by catcalls. The audience of educators began to hoot and holler and tell him to sit down.

One student stood to say, "Who's going to do the moral instructing?" Another argued, "Whose morality are we going to follow?" With that the audience thundered applause, and President Rhodes sat down, silenced.

No one even thought to answer, "If not biblical revelation, haven't we at least been able, throughout the long history of Western civilization, to rely on natural law?" No one even ventured such an answer. We have lost the capacity even to intelligently discuss moral and religious issues in culture.

Bryn Mawr political scientist Stephen Salkever was quoted in *Time* magazine recently, saying, "There was a traditional language of public discourse, based partly on biblical sources and partly on republican sources." But that language, says Salkever, has now fallen into disuse, leaving America without a way to communicate moral values.[3]

Why are we horrified at the growing consequences of sexual promiscuity, including a life-threatening epidemic—when sex is treated as casually as going out for a Frosty at Wendy's?

Why should it surprise us that Wall Street brokers trade for their own profit, bilking billions of dollars from the public—when there is no standard of right and wrong?

Why are we shocked when West Pointers and Marines

sell secrets for sexual gratification—if there is no honor, duty, or higher calling than one's own well-being?

If life has no meaning beyond self, why not exterminate the unwanted unborn or, for that matter, the inconvenient elderly?

Malcolm Muggeridge has a wonderful way of summing things up, and he recently wrote, "Just when happiness seems most accessible, in the happy lands—the Scandinavias and Californias—many jump after it from upstairs windows or gulp it down in colored barbiturates or try to tear it out of one another's bodies or scatter it in blood and bone on the highways, along which, with six lanes aside and Muzak endlessly playing, automobiles roll on from nowhere to nowhere."[4]

That is the vacuum in which we live. That is what happens when absolute right and wrong are removed from society. That is what happens when the prophecy of Nietzsche comes true, as it has come true in Western culture.

The Search for Ethics

But there is also good news. The good news is that for the first time the secular world is beginning to recognize what is happening. That is what the recent cover story of *Time* magazine was about: "What Ever Happened to Ethics?" That is why Harvard Business School is now revising its curriculum, struggling for how it can come to grips with ethical questions. That is why Secretary of Education William Bennett is touring this country, crusading for the need to put values back in education—and why many others are behind him, doing the same thing. That is what accounts for people like Ted Koppel saying in his magnificent speech at Duke University, "The Ten Commandments are *commandments*, not ten suggestions." That is what has caused people to begin to cry out against the values vacuum—a cry of the heart from the secular world.

But who should answer that cry?

The church, of course. The government is not going to be the propagator of moral values in society. There is no other institution anywhere that is capable of articulating a moral code by which we can live. It is the church of Jesus Christ alone which, proclaiming the revealed truths of Scripture, is able to provide values. It is able—but only if it will be the church, the people of God living by what the King teaches us about his kingdom.

But what has happened to the church? How have Christians responded? One thing some Christians have done is to retreat into spiritual ghettos, to *privatize their faith*. For these, the religious resurgence in America has been entirely of a personal nature. That one hour a week that they separate out for their quiet time has become the whole of their religious experience. They have made their experience with God just one part of life.

A second thing that has been done is to create what Dietrich Bonhoeffer referred to decades ago as *cheap grace*. We see it everywhere. Cheap grace makes no place for repentance. Cheap grace simply says, "Take whatever God will give you—and the more material blessings the better." Tammy Bakker has said, "When I ask God for a new car, I tell him the color I want." We laugh at that, but unfortunately there is much of that thinking in our pulpits and churches today.

None of us should be self-righteous about the PTL tragedy, because the sins of greed and fornication—the sins that caused that ministry to fall—can happen to any ministry. But, you know, I have come to believe that the root cause of the PTL tragedy—the *root* cause—was not so much greed, sexual temptation, or abuse of power. It was that Jim and Tammy Bakker began to preach a false "health and wealth" prosperity gospel and then, sadly, actually began to believe and practice it. That is the tragedy, in my opinion, and that is cheap grace. There is no place for it in the church of Jesus Christ.

The third thing besides being privatized and being afflicted with cheap grace, is that we have become *politicized*. It is good that many Christians are now entering the political arena. But never, never must we tie the gospel of Jesus Christ to anyone's political agenda. Peter Burger made a perceptive comment when writing about a cancer-stricken friend who was a member of a mainline, liberal church—though the same thing could have happened in a conservative church. He said when this man went to look for help from the clergy, all the ministers wanted to do was talk about Nicaragua, South Africa, and other social issues. This man was dying of cancer, and there was no one to talk to him. Burger concludes, "Whenever a political agenda is seen as constitutive of the church, all those who dissent from it are excluded from the church. And in that very instant, the church is no longer catholic. Indeed, it ceases to be the church."

One of our brethren, no doubt well-meaning and well-intentioned, recently said when a legislative program was defeated in Congress, "We have been legislated out of revival." Legislated out of revival? How can that be? The God I worship is stronger than the Congress of the United States.

The Coming of the Kingdom

Why has the church failed? In Luke 4 there is a story with which we are all doubtless familiar. Jesus entered the synagogue in his hometown, picked the book of Isaiah from the Torah shrine, unrolled it to chapter 61 and began to read. It was the first time he had returned to his hometown.

> "The Spirit of the Lord is on me,
> because he has anointed me
> to preach good news to the poor.
> He has sent me to proclaim freedom for the prisoners
> and recovery of sight for the blind,
> to release the oppressed,
> to proclaim the year of the Lord's favor.

Then he said, "Today this scripture is fulfilled in your hearing" (vv. 18-19, 21).

We have lost sight of what Jesus was saying in that synagogue. In those days there were Zealots who wanted a politicized faith as much as many today want a political solution to our problems. And there were Pharisees who had a privatized faith, just as many today also do. Jesus walked into a situation exactly like one he might find in an American church today. He could have picked any Scripture he wanted from the Old Testament. Why did he pick these particular verses?

For ten or eleven years, I have gone to prisons and have preached from Luke 4:18. The inmates love to hear about "freedom for . . . prisoners." And I have to confess that I have preached that verse as a message of human liberation. But as I began working on my new book about the kingdom of God, I came to understand what that message really means—and why Jesus took these verses from Isaiah 61 to define the nature of his ministry. Why? Because they are a prophetic description of the Messiah's empire. They are the declaration of the coming of the kingdom of God. What Jesus was saying was that "the kingdom has come *in me*."

The trouble with the church today is that we are treating Christianity as if it were just like the Buddhist or Hindu religions, or any other religion. But it is not. It is not a creed. It is not a set of beliefs. It is not a formula for better living. It is not a way to feel better. Christianity is Jesus Christ—and the message that the kingdom of God has come in him and will come in even greater fullness when he returns. That is a radical message. It is the most radical message I can imagine.

Edmund P. Clowney writes that this announcement of the kingdom by Jesus is the distinctive message of the Christian gospel, since the theology of the kingdom lies at the very heart of the New Testament revelation. Go back, as I have done, and read the New Testament again, tuning your mind to look for references to the kingdom. It will change your Christian faith. You will discover that virtually all the parables are related to the kingdom. You will find texts such as, "No one can see the kingdom of God unless he is born again. . . . No one can enter the kingdom of God" (John 3:3, 5). You will find that Jesus' miracles show his dominion over the earth and thus prove that the kingdom had come in him. You will hear him summing it up by saying, "Seek first his kingdom [the kingdom of God] and his righteousness, and all these [other] things will be given to you as well" (Matthew 6:33).

Jesus' first words, spoken in the synagogue of Nazareth, were not the announcement of an earthly political program. His inaugural speech was a deliberate announcement of the kingdom of God. We cannot help notice, however, that when he went on to explain the nature of the kingdom more fully, and when people understood that it was not just to be a kingdom for Jews—it was for everyone—they ran him out of the synagogue. His message did not satisfy the Pharisees. It did not satisfy the Zealots. It satisfied no one. Is it any different today? Unfortunately, if true Christianity were being preached today, and if people today really understood it, it would be run out of the churches in many parts of America in our time, just as in that first and formative incident.

Why is the announcement of the kingdom such a radical message? It is radical because, first of all, it puts us in a very difficult position. Jesus announced the kingdom, but it is a kingdom that has not yet come in its fullness, and, as a result, we live in tension. We live by the commandments of God as citizens of the kingdom of God. But we also live in the midst of the fallen kingdoms of this world.

How do we survive in this tension? We survive because we know the final chapter of the story. We live in the midst of pain, stress, strain, sin, horror, and degradation, but we know that the kingdom of God is not of this world. It is transcendent and, thus, more powerful. It is not a realm. It is far more. It is a rule, the rule of God over all things—men and nations. It is to that rule that we must swear allegiance as citizens of the kingdom of God. That is what Jesus is calling us to do.

When we talk like this, people will justly say to us, "Of what earthly use is this heavenly kingdom?" It is of much earthly use, for at least the following five reasons.

Best of Citizens

The secular world is scared to death of Christians. They are scared that we are going to impose our views on them, cramming them down their throats. They think that we are a bunch of Bible-pounding bigots. But if they really understood what it means to be a citizen of the kingdom of God, they would welcome us with open arms because, as Augustine argued, the citizens of the kingdom of God should be the best of citizens of the kingdoms of this world. That is because we do out of the love of God what others do only out of the threat and force of law. This enables Christians to rise above their natural egoism. And this is why, in the nineteenth century, the great social reforms were brought about by Christians. That is why in England the slave trade was abolished by William Wilberforce—because Christians could rise above their self-interest and be the best of citizens, doing what they did, not by force of law but out of love of God. We should be the most responsible of citizens.

Instruments of Forgiveness

Second, being a citizen of the kingdom of God is the only way in which the cycle of evil and violence in the world can be broken.

I am a baseball fan, and I recall reading something that happened when the Detroit Tigers and the New York Yankees were in a heated contest for the American League East lead last summer. George Steinbrenner was outraged that the Tigers would not let their star pitcher pitch in the All-Star game because they did not want him to miss his regular rotation. Steinbrenner was quoted in the press as saying, "That's the rottenest thing I've ever heard of, and we're going to do it next year." That is the nature of man which ensures the perpetuation of the cycle of evil.

Some religions teach that we are bound by this cycle. Hinduism says that whatever evil you do in this life will be done to you in the next life, which is simply a way of perpetuating evil. There is no escape from it. Can anything break this cycle? What breaks it is the reconciling love of Jesus Christ which alone enables us to turn the other cheek and forgive. A citizen of the kingdom of God can be an instrument of such forgiveness.

I have been to Belfast, Ireland, where Catholics and
Protestants have been killing one another for decades. I have
taken born-again Catholic and Protestant lads out of prison,
brought them onto a platform, and there they have put their
arms around one another and proclaimed their new brotherhood.
They have said—as two did at our conference there a few years
ago— "Once I would have killed this man, but today I would
lay my life down for him because he's my brother." If there is
hope for the kingdoms of man, it is because the citizens of
God's kingdom are able to practice such love and reconciliation.

Victory Over Crime

Third, citizens of the kingdom of God in the midst of the
kingdoms of man provide domestic tranquillity.

I deal in the area of crime. Everybody believes that crime
is caused by economic and sociological factors, particularly
poverty. But it is simply not true. Rather, as Professor James
Wilson at Harvard discovered, there is an extraordinary inverse
correlation between crime and religious activity. He discovered
that every time there has been an upsurge of religious activity—
genuine spiritual revival—in American history, crime has dropped. It is in times of spiritual poverty, not times of economic
poverty, that crime goes up.

Wilson found, for example, a correlation between the
Victorian values of the nineteenth century and the decline of
crime. At a very time when rapid urbanization should have
caused more crime according to modern theories, Victorian
values actually caused crime to drop.

And in 1904, when there was a great revival in Wales,
the social effects were dramatic. Profanity disappeared from
the coal mines. Crime rates dropped so suddenly that many
policemen were unemployed. Court calendars were cleared up,
and judges had little work.

Do you want to stop crime in this country? It's not going
to be accomplished by building more prisons. It is going to be
accomplished only as people's hearts are changed as the result

of a genuine spiritual movement, a movement which comes from Christians living by the law of another kingdom, the kingdom of God.

Divine Law beyond Human Law

Fourth, the citizens of the kingdom of God living in the midst of the kingdoms of the world provide a respect for the Law that stands beyond human law. It means the presence of a community of people whose values are established by eternal truths. There is no other place that a culture can find those values.

I said earlier that when President Rhodes of Cornell spoke for moral values and was hooted down, someone should have stood up and said, "How about natural law?" But I need to add that, after that was done, someone should have stood up—though he or she would probably have been tarred and feathered if he or she had done it—and said, "How about the revealed propositional truth of Scripture, because that is the Law that is beyond law?" The Bible provides a basis for absolute truth, for true right and true wrong. It is only the citizens of the kingdom in the midst of the kingdoms of man that make that discovery possible.

God's "Little Platoons"

The fifth benefit of citizenship in the kingdom of God in the midst of the kingdoms of man is what happens when Christians, motivated by the love of God, band together in what Edmund Burke called "the little platoons"—not the big institutions, but the little platoons of people who gather together to do the little, often simple things that need to be done.

Congress on the Bible II was responsible for one example, as people who came to the congress got together to repair and paint a home for needy persons in the nation's capital.

In Philadelphia an eleven-year-old lad named Trevor Ferrell turned on the television set and saw homeless people sleeping on the streets. He took a blanket off his bed, turned to his parents and said, "Daddy and Mommy can we take this down and give it to those homeless people?" That started a whole movement of Christians going into downtown Philadelphia to give people blankets, find places for them to sleep, feed them, and build shelters.

A California woman by the name of Frieda Weststeyn lived near a women's prison and saw that there was no place for the children of the inmates. So she took several into her home, and they lived with her. She had four until the state came in and said arbitrarily that she could only keep three. She gave the women's children a place to live.

John Perkins, a successful businessman in California, went back to Mendenhall, Mississippi, his hometown, and started a self-help movement among his people. "No government welfare," they said. "We'll do it ourselves." And they did! They started a clinic and a co-op. I have been there to visit them. It is the little platoons of God's people that get action.

Jerry Falwell was preaching about abortion one day and was deeply convicted because a reporter said to him, "It's all well and good to preach against abortion, but what about these poor pregnant women? Who will help them?" So Falwell started a home for pregnant women as part of Liberty University. His "Save-a-Baby Program" is now in six hundred cities across America. These Christians are reaching out—not simply denouncing abortion but holding out a loving hand to those who are in that condition.

My friend, Jack Eckerd, the very first day after he became a Christian walked into one of his drug stores—there are seventeen hundred of them across the United States—and saw *Playboy* and *Penthouse* on the magazine racks. He went back to his president and said, "Take those out of the stores."

When I read about that I called him and said, "Jack, did you do that because you have become a Christian?"

He said, "Why else would I throw away three million dollars?"

When he did that, Seven-Eleven followed suit, and today eleven thousand stores across America are free of pornography—without a single law being passed. Those are the little platoons at work.

I was in Africa last summer at the Prison Fellowship International Congress. A man came to it from Madagascar, where he had been a professor of entomology at the University of Madagascar. When there was a Marxist coup, he was thrown in prison. Earlier he had renounced his youthful allegiance to Christ, because in academic circles in Madagascar a person is simply not accepted as a Christian. But in prison Jesus came to him, and this professor began to preach the gospel. He began to build a Christian fellowship inside that prison.

Then one day last year, after he had been released from prison, he was walking by the prison yard and saw sixty corpses on the prison infirmary steps. He was shocked. He went in and asked, "What happened? Is there a plague?"

The nurse said, "No, that is just the number of people who die here every week because we have rations for twenty-five hundred inmates but actually house five thousand. Fifty to seventy starve to death every week."

The man went home that night and told his wife, "We've got to do something." There was no World Vision, no big Christian organization to help him, no celebrities. He was just an ordinary person. There was nothing he could do but trust God and do what the Bible commands. So he and his wife began to cook. Today they cook rice and vegetable soup every week. They take them to the prison and keep seven hundred inmates alive.

The little platoons do not wait for somebody else to do Jesus' work. They do not expect it to be done by some big institution or celebrity. They do it because they know that the work of the kingdom must be done by the citizens of the kingdom and that, if we do it, each one of us, God will use us in ways we do not expect.

Citizens of the Kingdom

If we are to be true citizens of the kingdom, there are four requirements I urge us all to think about. The first is that *we must adhere scrupulously to orthodox, historic, classical Christian truth.* Donald Bloesch argued in his book, *Crumbling Foundations,* that secularism advances only as fast as orthodoxy retreats. I am not talking about dry dogma. Orthodoxy is the living truth that Jesus is the Son of God, was born of the virgin Mary, was fully God and fully man, was resurrected bodily; that the Bible is the holy, authoritative, inerrant Word of God; that Jesus will come again. That is orthodoxy. We must never sell it short. Sell that short, and we have nothing.

Second, *we must apply God's laws.* To know the laws of the kingdom is one thing, but then to apply the laws is the real test. We begin to do that only as we learn to think as Christians. Harry Blamires, the British critic, says, "There is no longer a Christian mind." I am inclined to agree with him. When you can have a gathering of educators like the one at Harvard, and nobody can even stand up and say, "How about natural law?" we are not thinking Christianly.

Recently I addressed the Texas legislature. I do not know how many of you have seen state legislatures, but it is a miracle that democracy somehow survives anyway. When I was there they were milling all over the place, and nobody could get their attention. The Speaker was rapping the gavel, but they did not respond. He said, "Don't worry, Chuck. George Bush was here two weeks ago, and they didn't pay any attention to him either." So I just started speaking. All of a sudden, these legislators started crowding in and sitting down. A hush came over the place. (I have discovered that politicians have a keen interest in prisons these days.) I told them that the only answer to the crime problem is to take nonviolent criminals out of our prisons and make them pay back their victims with restitution. That is how we can solve the prison crowding problem.

The amazing thing was that afterwards they came up to me one after another and said things like, "That's a tremendous idea. Why hasn't anyone thought of that?" I had the privilege of saying to them, "Read Exodus 22. It is only what God said to Moses on Mount Sinai thousands of years ago."

Do not try to hit secular people over the head with a Bible. They are not going to listen to it. Rather, argue your case, and then point out that the point you are making is grounded in the wisdom of Scripture. Think Christianly, because as we think Christianly we will act Christianly.

Third, *fulfill your civic duty by being part of a little platoon*. This means getting out of our pews. See what a difference you will make. You will be amazed. The story of the ministry that I am part of, Prison Fellowship, is one of ordinary people doing extraordinary things by the power of God.

Fourth, *do not be taken in by the political illusion* . Realize that being a citizen of the kingdom of God means that you are a citizen of the kingdom of God first, and a citizen of this world second. Yes, we obey the laws of earthly kingdoms in submission to earthly authorities. We are commanded to, and we know that governments are ordained by God to preserve order. But we must never put the governments of men on the same level as the government of God.

A few years ago, I was getting on an airplane and an oriental-looking man got out of his seat very excitedly as I was walking down the aisle. He grabbed me and said, "Chuck Colson, Chuck Colson, I . . ."

I said, "Please sit down. Sit down." He was so excited.

I did not know where he came from, but he began to tell me. "I was in prison for seven years and seven months. Someone gave me your book. I was converted by reading your book."

Again I said, "Please sit down. We are holding up people who are trying to get on the airplane."

Then he told me his name: Benino Aquino.

That was in 1981. We became good friends. In 1983, he called me and said, "I am going back to the Philippines, Chuck."

"But you might be put in prison," I protested.

"I'm not worried," he said. "If Marcos puts me in prison, I'll head Prison Fellowship within the prison. If they have elections, I'll be elected president of the Philippines. If they kill me, I'll be with Jesus. It won't matter."

He went back. You know the story. He arrived at the airport, stepped off the plane but never got to the tarmac, because he was shot and killed at that moment. An assassin's bullet stopped Benino Aquino. But it did not stop what he stood for. A movement began which spread all through the Philippines. Bible studies started springing up, both Protestant and Catholic. Cardinal Sin traveled around the Philippines telling people that they needed to be born again, that they needed to repent of their sin and come to Jesus. So when the election was held in February a year ago and Marcos stole it from Cory Aquino, Benino's widow, three hundred soldiers and two generals announced a revolution. Cardinal Sin went on the radio and said, "All nuns and priests, go into the churches and convents and pray with your hands stretched up to God until God delivers this nation. All other Christians, go out on the street." Within thirty minutes, two million Philippine citizens—Protestant and Catholic—were out on the street, kneeling and praying in front of the tanks. The tanks could not move. The army was stopped. Democracy was restored. And not a drop of blood was shed.

Don't tell me that the armies or politicians of this world are stronger than the power of God. They are not. The political illusion springs from a diminished belief in God and the growth of big government. What people once expected from an Almighty God they now expect from an almighty bureaucracy. And that is a bad trade.

If ever you are in Washington, D.C., I want you to do something. I want you to take a walk, preferably at night. I want you to walk down to Pennsylvania Avenue and look up Pennsylvania Avenue to the east. You will see the Capitol sparkling in the night light. Then look the other way. You will see the White House, that majestic building. If you look a little to the left, you will see the Washington Monument towering into the sky, and beyond it the Lincoln Memorial in the distance. I think it is the most beautiful of all the monuments in Washington. If you walk down to the ellipse, you will be able to see them all at one time. It is one of the most glorious views in the world.

But as you look, realize that no human kingdom has ever survived. Realize the truth of what Augustine said, that the city of man is built by man and will be destroyed by man, but that the city of God endures forever because it is built by God. Look at those buildings and know that one day—glorious though they are and as much as they mean to us—one day they will remain only as ruins. Stand in the still night air. If you stand there long enough and listen hard enough, I think in the distance you might hear the refrain of the "Hallelujah Chorus" from Handel's great oratorio, *Messiah.* The words are from Revelation:

> "The kingdom of the world has become the kingdom
> of our Lord and of His Christ,
> and he will reign for ever and ever."
>
> (Revelation 11:15)

That is our hope. Hallelujah!

Chapter 9, Notes

1. Historical details taken from William Manchester, *American Caesar: Douglas MacArthur 1880-1964* (Boston: Little, Brown, 1978), quotes from pp. 452-54.

2. Quoted in David Brock, "A Philosopher Hurls Down a Stinging Moral Gauntlet," *Insight,* 11 May 1987, 12.

3. "Ethics: Looking to Its Roots," *Time,* 25 May 1987, 26.

4. Malcolm Muggeridge, *The Portable Conservative Reader* (New York: Penguin Books, 1982), 617.

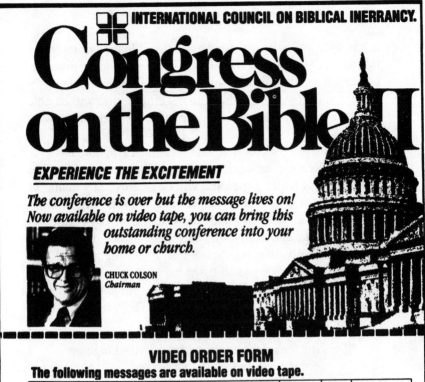

▧▧ INTERNATIONAL COUNCIL ON BIBLICAL INERRANCY.

Congress on the Bible II

EXPERIENCE THE EXCITEMENT

The conference is over but the message lives on! Now available on video tape, you can bring this outstanding conference into your home or church.

CHUCK COLSON
Chairman

VIDEO ORDER FORM

The following messages are available on video tape.

	TAPE	QUANTITY	COST	TOTAL
#1	One Nation Under God—*James Boice*		$17.50	$
#2	The Christian and Society—*Os Guinness* The Christian and the Sanctity of Life—*R. C. Sproul*		$35.00	$
#3	The Christian and God's World—*J.I. Packer* The Christian and the Church—*Richard John Neuhaus*		$35.00	$
#4	The Inseparability of Reality and Ideals—*Sen. Wm. Armstrong* The Christian and Biblical Justice—*John M. Perkins*		$35.00	$
#5	The Inseparability of Church and State—*William Buckley, Jr.* The Kingdom of God and Human Kingdoms—*Charles W. Colson*		$35.00	$
#6	Complete Set		$100.	$
		TOTAL		$

Please send to:

Name _____

Street _____

City/State/Zip _____

Phone _____

☐ Charge to: VISA # _____   MasterCard # _____

Exp. date: _____   ☐ Enclosed is my check.   FORMAT ☐ VHS ☐ BETA

Mail To: Ligonier Ministries, P.O. Box 7500, Orlando, FL 32854
Or Call: 1-800-435-4343 · Florida Residents: 407-834-1633